Ready-to-Go
U.S.
Outline Maps

S C H O L A S T I C
PROFESSIONAL BOOKS

New York • Toronto • London • Auckland • Sydney
Mexico City • New Delhi • Hong Kong

Cover design by Jaime Lucero and Kelli Thompson
Interior design by Norma Ortiz
Maps by Mapquest.com

ISBN 0-439-11762-3

Table of Contents

Introduction

The outline maps in this book are an instant way for you to help your students become geography-wise. You simply reproduce the maps, and you and your students are ready to use them in reports, for bulletin board displays, and for all kinds of activities and projects.

Using the maps will also help you to meet the National Geography Standards, in particular, Standard 1, which states:

The geographically informed person knows and understands:

Knowledge Standard I – How to use maps and other geographic representations, tools, and technologies to acquire, process, and report information from a spatial perspective.

Supply List

You may want to have the following supplies available for the activities and projects.

Scissors

Glue sticks

Construction paper

White paper

Stapler and staples

Crayons, colored pencils, markers

Paper fasteners

Tagboard or file folders

Envelopes of various sizes

Yarn in different colors

But using these maps will also help your students meet other standards. For example, Standard 2 states that students should know and understand the physical and human characteristics of places. When students use the base outline map to make a product map or a landform map, they are developing these understandings.

Since we use maps all the time in the real world, all students will benefit from understanding how to read and use them. And maps are also fun! A few suggestions for using the maps are included on pages 7-10.

Reports

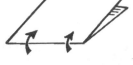

Students can use the outline maps in a number of ways when they're doing reports about the states. Encourage them to use the base outline map as a starting point for creating maps that give a more complete picture of the state. They can add symbols to make a produce or resource map, for example. They can include illustrations and photos showing important landforms or tourist sites. Invite them to create their own symbols, or they can use some that are provided in the box on this page. Remind them to include a map key to explain the symbols.

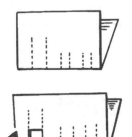

Reports don't have to flat! Students will be eager to write reports when they are 3-D. Show them how to make pop-up reports by making a pop-up tab (see illustration and photos).

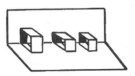

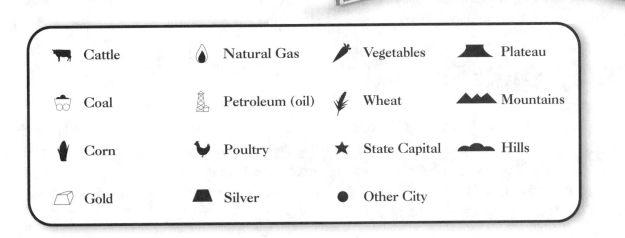

🐄 Cattle	🛢 Natural Gas	🥕 Vegetables	◣ Plateau
⛑ Coal	🛢 Petroleum (oil)	🌾 Wheat	⛰ Mountains
🌽 Corn	🐔 Poultry	★ State Capital	⌒ Hills
💎 Gold	◼ Silver	● Other City	

Mystery Envelopes

In this activity, students use a series of clues to determine which of the 50 states is being described. Place a copy of a state outline map in an 8 1/2- by 11-inch envelope. On the outside of the envelope, write, or have students write, three clues about the state. The clues can also be illustrations or photos. Laminating the envelopes will make them sturdier. Punch a hole in the corner of the envelopes and use a metal ring to keep them all together. Students need to read the clues and decide which state is hidden in side.

Scrambled States Pictures

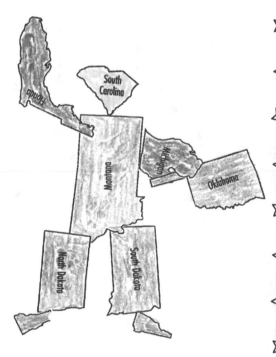

The results of this fun activity make a great bulletin board display. Have copies of the outline maps available to students. Explain that they can use the maps to create pictures. Have them cut out the states they want to use and arrange them to make a picture. They should use a state only once. When they have finished arranging the states, have them color in their creations. Suggest that they include an imaginative title or caption. Finally, tell students to make a list of all the states they used in their picture. Hang the finished pictures on a bulletin board. You may want to have on hand the book *The Scrambled States of America* by Laurie Keller.

Map Book

Provide students with several copies of a state outline map. Invite them to use the maps to show different things about the state. For example, they can show large cities, or popular tourist destinations, or interesting landforms and bodies of water. They may want to create a personal map that shows where they live and the places they've visited in the state. Compile all the maps into a class map book.

Map Quilt

Decide on a subject for your quilt. It could be the entire U.S., or just a region. Have each student select a state or states. Explain that they will use the map to make a quilt square for a class quilt. Have them color in the map, highlighting important places. Then have them paste each map to a piece of construction paper. Alternate the colors of the background paper. Tape each of the pieces of construction paper together to make a map paper quilt to display on a bulletin board.

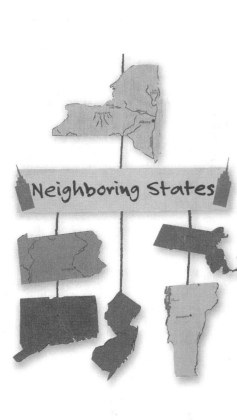

Map Mobile

Invite students to make map mobiles that show the relationships among places. For example, a mobile might show the states that neighbor the state students live in, or states that border the Atlantic Ocean or Mississippi River. To make the mobile, have them select and prepare the state outline maps they want to use. Have them color and cut out the maps. Then have them create a header card that includes an appropriate label. Have them use a hole puncher and yarn to connect the states they've selected to the header card.

Fan Book

Have students use the fact sheet on page 10 to collect information about their state or a state they are studying. Then have them color the map of the state. Next, have them paste the map and fact sheet to a piece of tagboard, or a file folder. (A legal-size folder works best.) They should paste the map and fact sheet down so the map is above the fact sheet (see photo), and then cut them out as one piece. Have students use these pages to create fan books. You might have them create a fan page for all the states in your region, or all the states that neighbor your state. Attach the pages with a paper fastener and include a first page with a title.

Name_____ Date _____

State Facts

After you fill in the blanks, cut out the fact sheet. Follow your teacher's instructions for adding a map at the top.

State _____

Origin of Name _____

Capital _____

Admitted to the Union _____

Motto _____

Song _____

Flower _____

Bird _____

Tree _____

Major Cities _____

_____

Major Rivers _____

_____

Goods and Services _____

_____

_____

U.S. Outline Maps

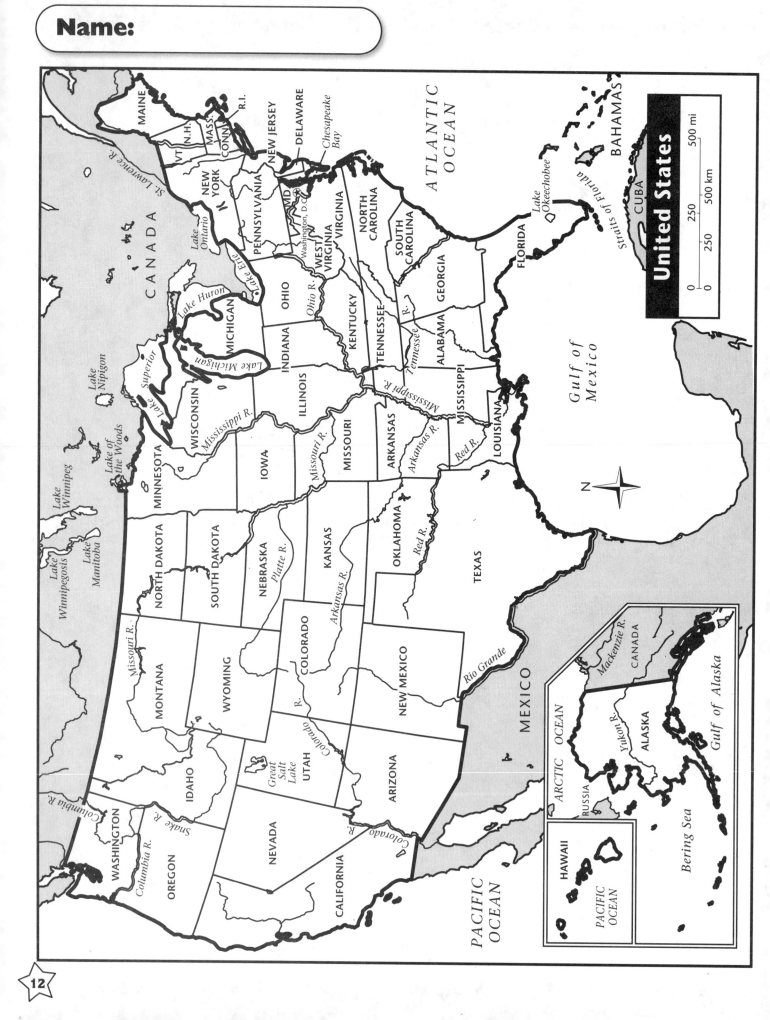

United States

ATLANTIC OCEAN

PACIFIC OCEAN

Gulf of Mexico

CANADA

MEXICO

BAHAMAS

CUBA

MAINE
N.H.
VT
MASS.
R.I.
CONN.
NEW YORK
NEW JERSEY
DELAWARE
PENNSYLVANIA
MD
Washington, D.C.
WEST VIRGINIA
VIRGINIA
NORTH CAROLINA
SOUTH CAROLINA
GEORGIA
FLORIDA
OHIO
INDIANA
KENTUCKY
TENNESSEE
ALABAMA
MISSISSIPPI
LOUISIANA
MICHIGAN
WISCONSIN
ILLINOIS
IOWA
MISSOURI
ARKANSAS
MINNESOTA
NORTH DAKOTA
SOUTH DAKOTA
NEBRASKA
KANSAS
OKLAHOMA
TEXAS
COLORADO
NEW MEXICO
WYOMING
MONTANA
IDAHO
UTAH
ARIZONA
NEVADA
CALIFORNIA
OREGON
WASHINGTON

Chesapeake Bay
Lake Okeechobee
Straits of Florida

St. Lawrence R.
Lake Ontario
Lake Erie
Lake Huron
Lake Michigan
Lake Superior
Lake Nipigon
Lake Winnipeg
Lake Manitoba
Lake Winnipegosis
Lake of the Woods

Ohio R.
Tennessee R.
Mississippi R.
Missouri R.
Arkansas R.
Red R.
Platte R.
Colorado R.
Rio Grande
Great Salt Lake
Snake R.
Columbia R.

N

500 mi
250
0
500 km
250
0

Inset map:

ARCTIC OCEAN
RUSSIA
CANADA
ALASKA
HAWAII
PACIFIC OCEAN
Bering Sea
Gulf of Alaska
Mackenzie R.
Yukon R.

Bering Strait

Bering Sea

Beaufort Sea

Baffin Bay

Denmark Strait

Yukon R.

Davis Strait

Gulf of Alaska

Mackenzie R.

Great Bear Lake

Labrador Sea

Great Slave Lake

Lake Athabasca

Hudson Bay

Peace R.

Athabasca R.

James Bay

Fraser R.

Columbia R.

Saskatchewan R.

Lake Winnipeg

St. Lawrence R.

N

Snake R.

Missouri R.

Lake Superior

L. Huron

Lake Ontario

Lake Michigan

L. Erie

Great Salt Lake

PACIFIC
OCEAN

Colorado R.

Platte R.

Ohio R.

Arkansas R.

Mississippi R.

ATLANTIC
OCEAN

Rio Grande

Gulf of Mexico

Bay of Campeche

Balsas

Caribbean Sea

Lake Nicaragua

PACIFIC
OCEAN

HAWAII

| 0 | 100 | 200 mi |
| 0 | 100 200 km | |

North America

| 0 | 200 | 400 | 600 | 800 mi |
| 0 | 400 | 800 km | | |

13

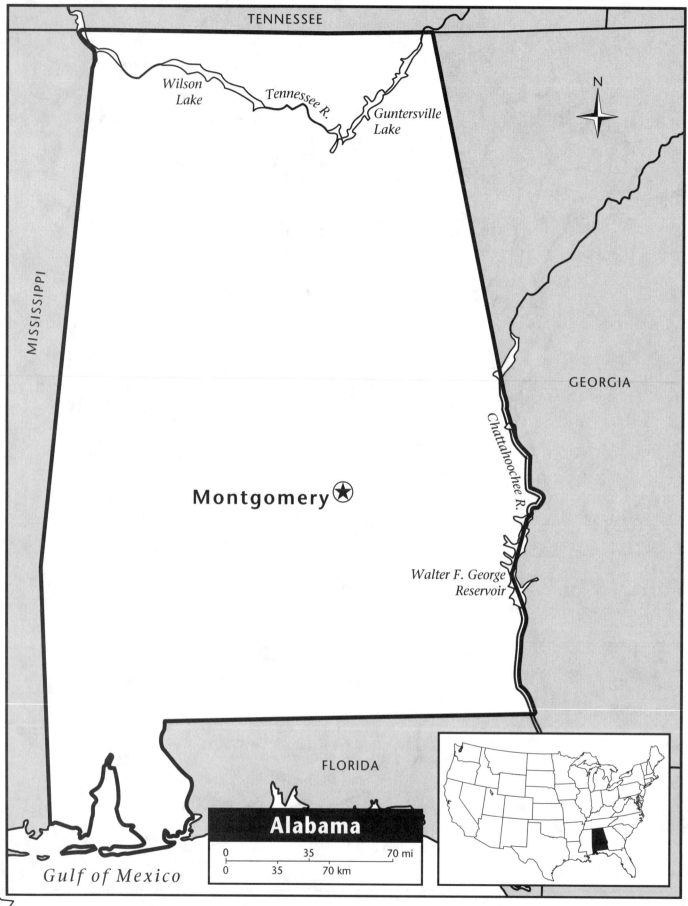

TENNESSEE

Wilson
Lake

Tennessee R.

Guntersville
Lake

N

MISSISSIPPI

GEORGIA

Chattahoochee R.

Montgomery ★

Walter F. George
Reservoir

FLORIDA

Alabama

| 0 | 35 | 70 mi |
| 0 | 35 | 70 km |

Gulf of Mexico

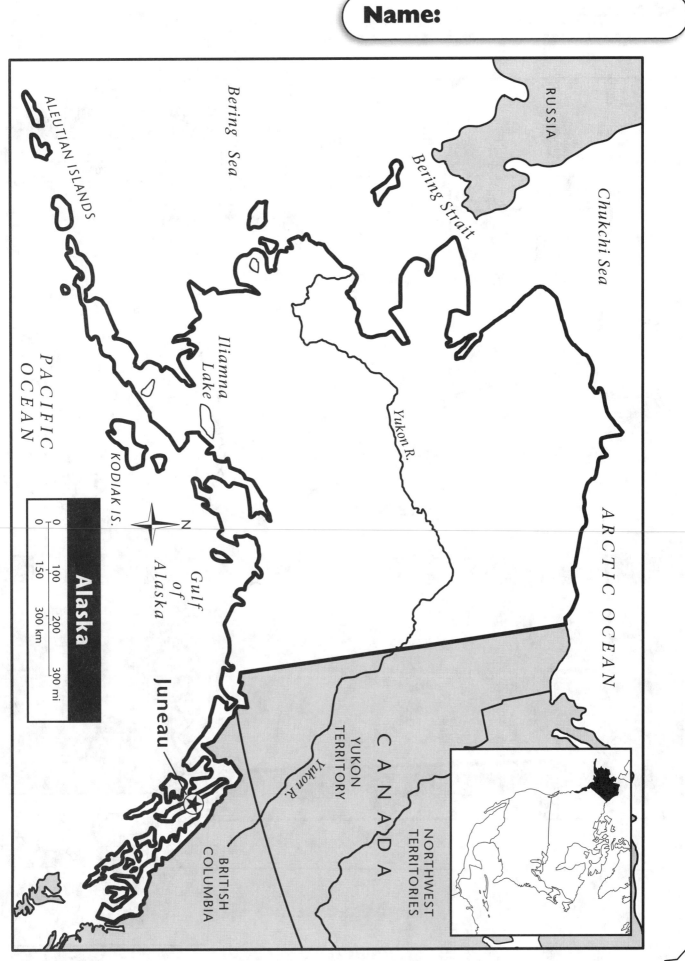

ALEUTIAN ISLANDS

RUSSIA

Bering Sea

Bering Strait

Chukchi Sea

Iliamna Lake

Yukon R.

PACIFIC OCEAN

KODIAK IS.

N

Gulf of Alaska

Alaska

0   100   200   300 km
0   150   300 mi

Juneau

ARCTIC OCEAN

CANADA

YUKON TERRITORY

Yukon R.

BRITISH COLUMBIA

NORTHWEST TERRITORIES

15

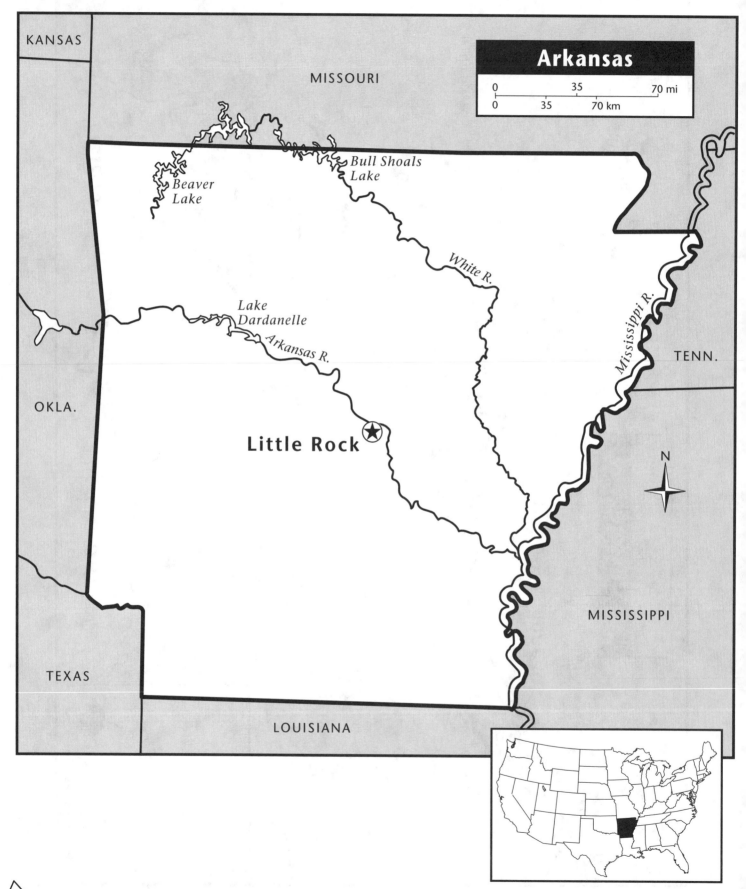

KANSAS

MISSOURI

Arkansas

| 0 | | 35 | | 70 mi |
| 0 | 35 | | 70 km | |

Bull Shoals Lake

Beaver Lake

White R.

Lake Dardanelle

Arkansas R.

Mississippi R.

OKLA.

TENN.

★ **Little Rock**

MISSISSIPPI

TEXAS

LOUISIANA

N

16

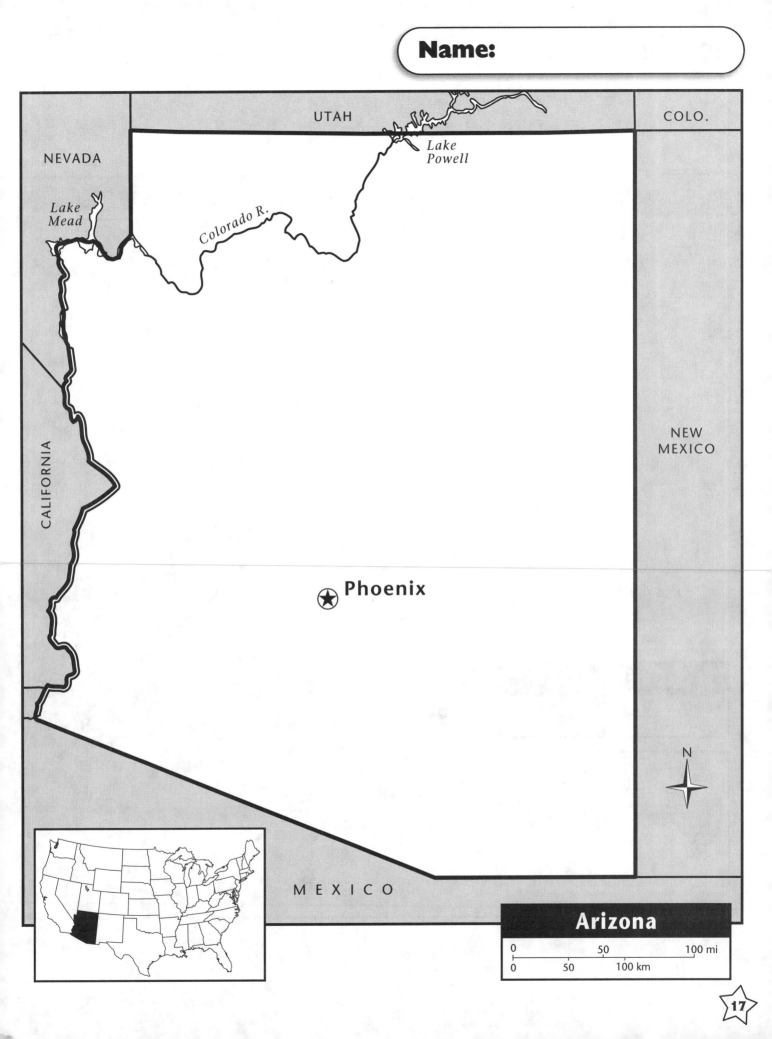

UTAH

COLO.

NEVADA

Lake Powell

Lake Mead

Colorado R.

CALIFORNIA

NEW MEXICO

⭐ **Phoenix**

N

MEXICO

Arizona

0		50		100 mi
0	50		100 km	

N

Klamath R.   Goose L.   OREGON

UTAH

Sacramento R.

Pyramid L.

NEVADA

L. Tahoe

★ **Sacramento**

San Joaquin R.

PACIFIC
OCEAN

L. Mead

California

| 0 | 75 | 150 mi |
| 0 | 75 | 150 km |

ARIZ.

Colorado R.

CHANNEL ISLANDS

Salton
Sea

MEXICO

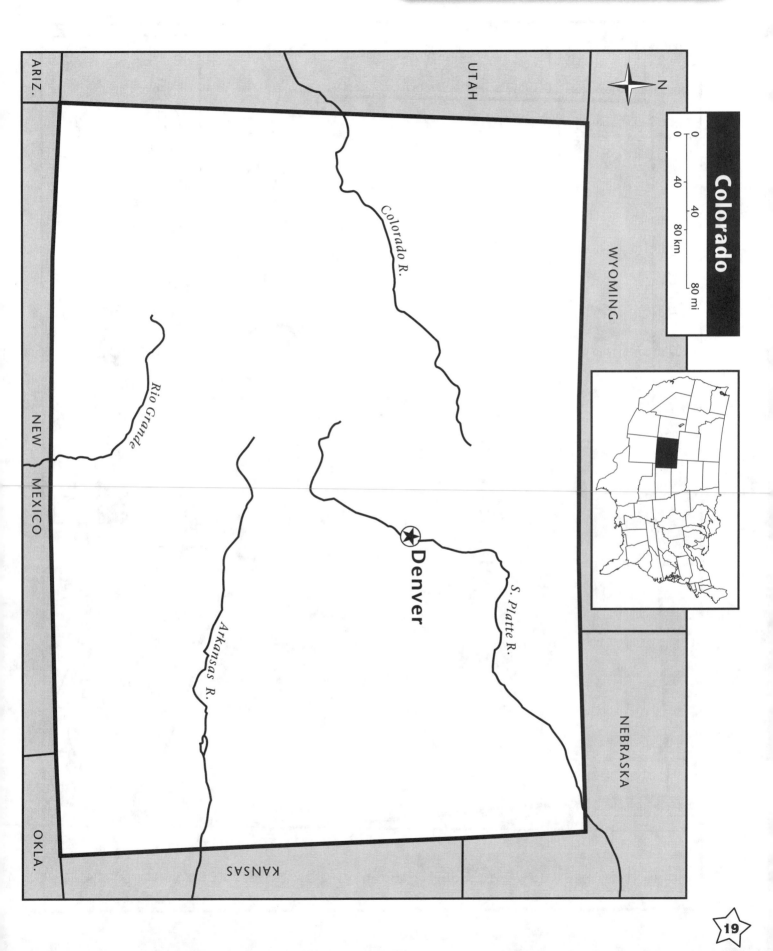

Colorado

ARIZ.

UTAH

N

0 40 80 km
0 40 80 mi

Colorado

WYOMING

Colorado R.

Rio Grande

NEW MEXICO

Arkansas R.

Denver

S. Platte R.

NEBRASKA

OKLA.

KANSAS

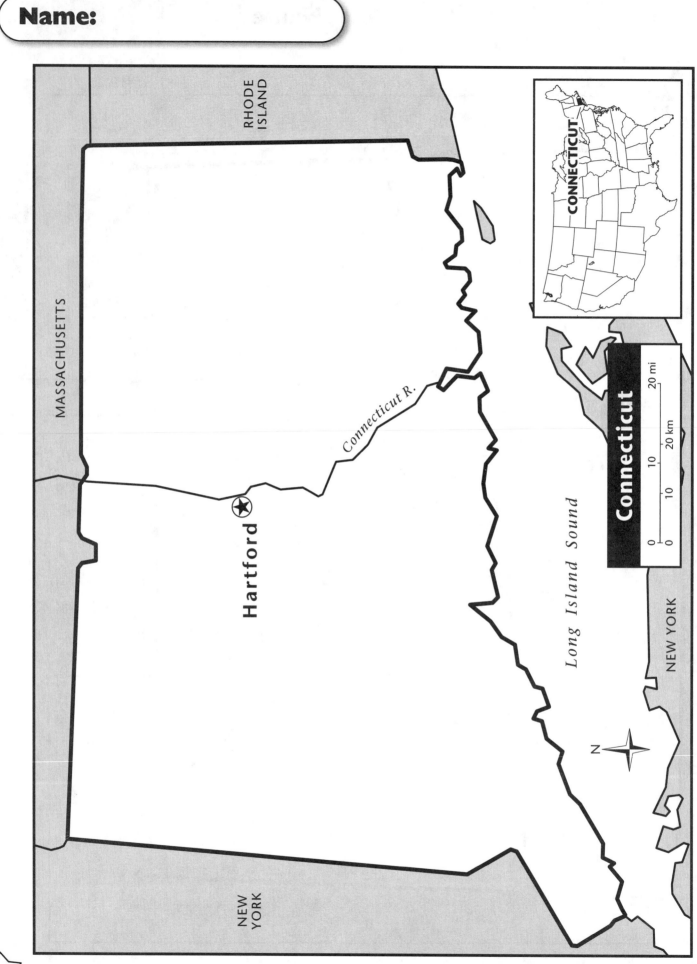

RHODE ISLAND

MASSACHUSETTS

Connecticut R.

Hartford

Long Island Sound

Connecticut

0   10   20 mi

0   10   20 km

NEW YORK

N

NEW YORK

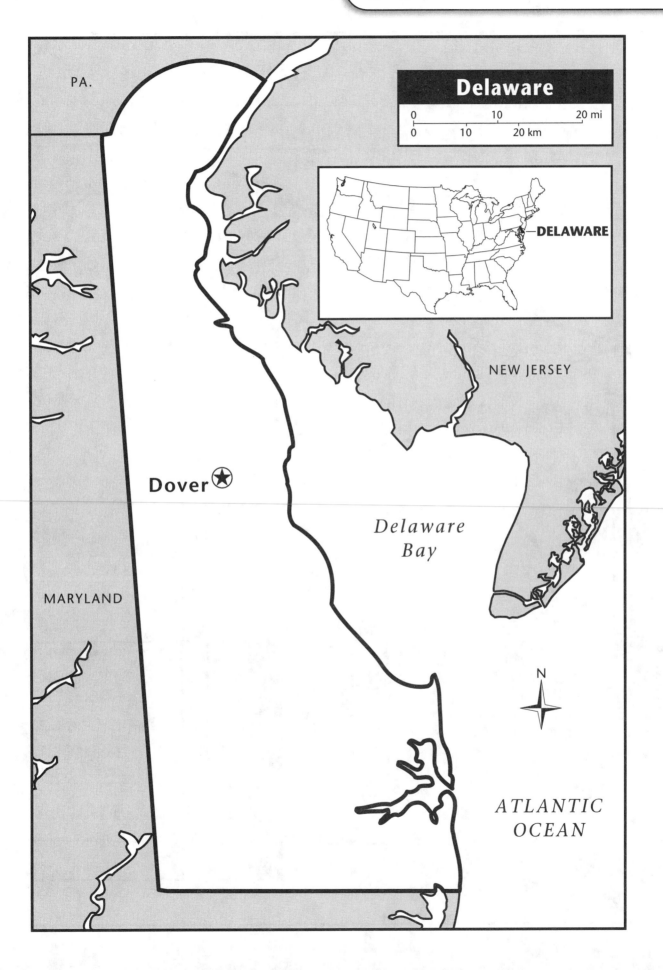

Delaware

0   10   20 mi
0   10   20 km

DELAWARE

PA.

MARYLAND

Dover ⭐

NEW JERSEY

Delaware
Bay

N

ATLANTIC
OCEAN

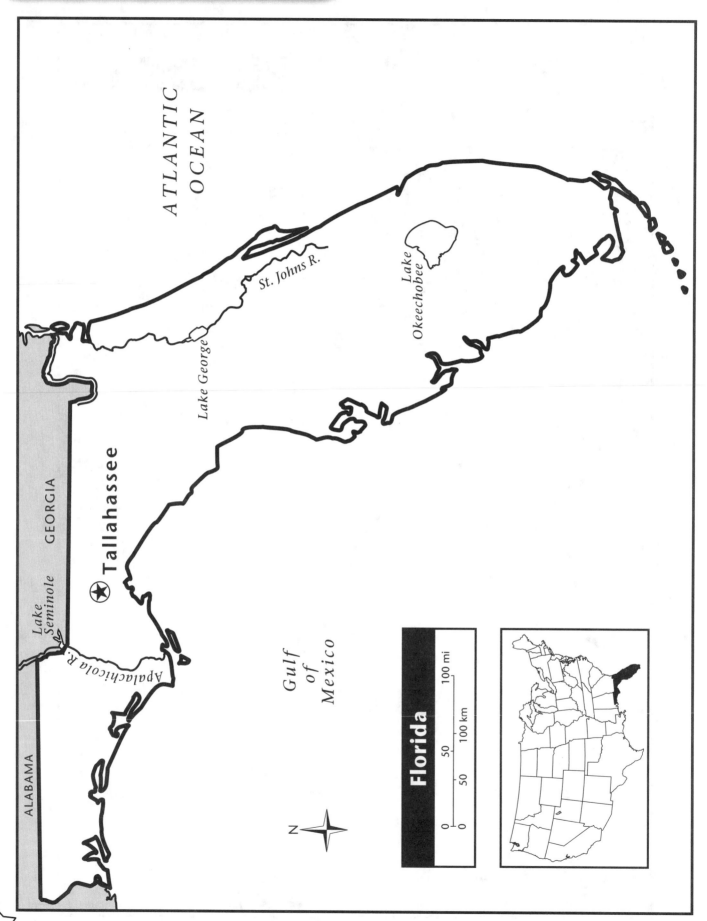

ATLANTIC OCEAN

St. Johns R.

Lake Okeechobee

Lake George

Tallahassee

GEORGIA

ALABAMA

Lake Seminole

Apalachicola R.

Gulf of Mexico

N

Florida

0   50   100 mi
0   50   100 km

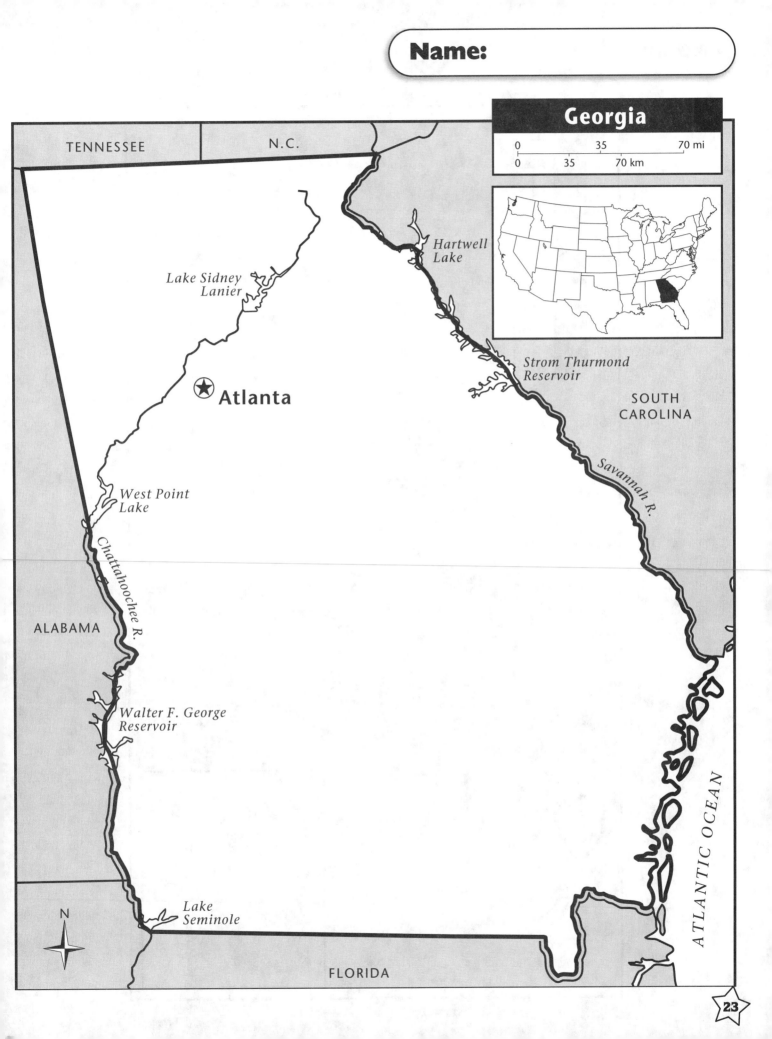

Georgia

0   35   70 mi
0   35   70 km

TENNESSEE

N.C.

Hartwell Lake

Lake Sidney Lanier

⭐ **Atlanta**

Strom Thurmond Reservoir

SOUTH CAROLINA

Savannah R.

West Point Lake

Chattahoochee R.

ALABAMA

Walter F. George Reservoir

ATLANTIC OCEAN

N

Lake Seminole

FLORIDA

23

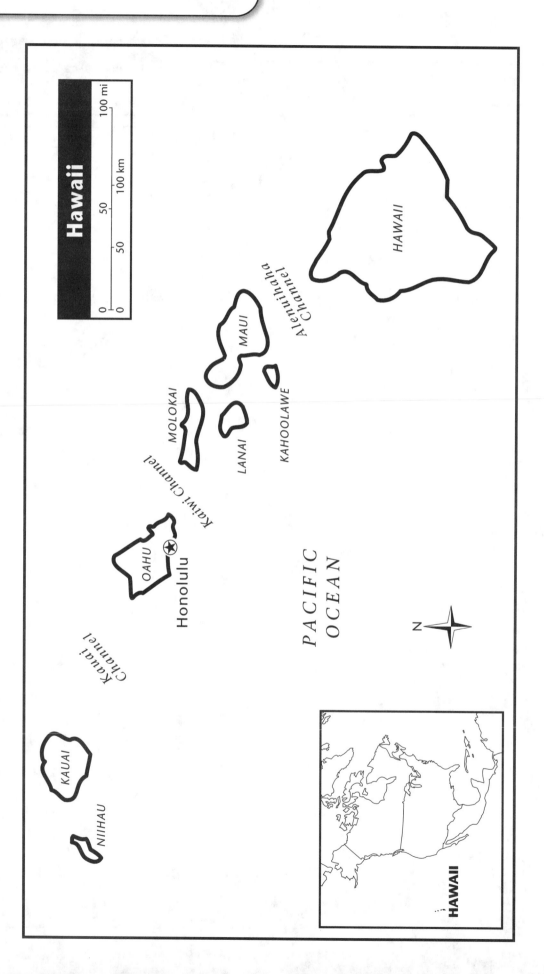

Hawaii

HAWAII

MAUI

Alenuihaha Channel

MOLOKAI

LANAI

KAHOOLAWE

Kaiwi Channel

OAHU

Honolulu

PACIFIC OCEAN

N

Kauai Channel

KAUAI

NIIHAU

HAWAII

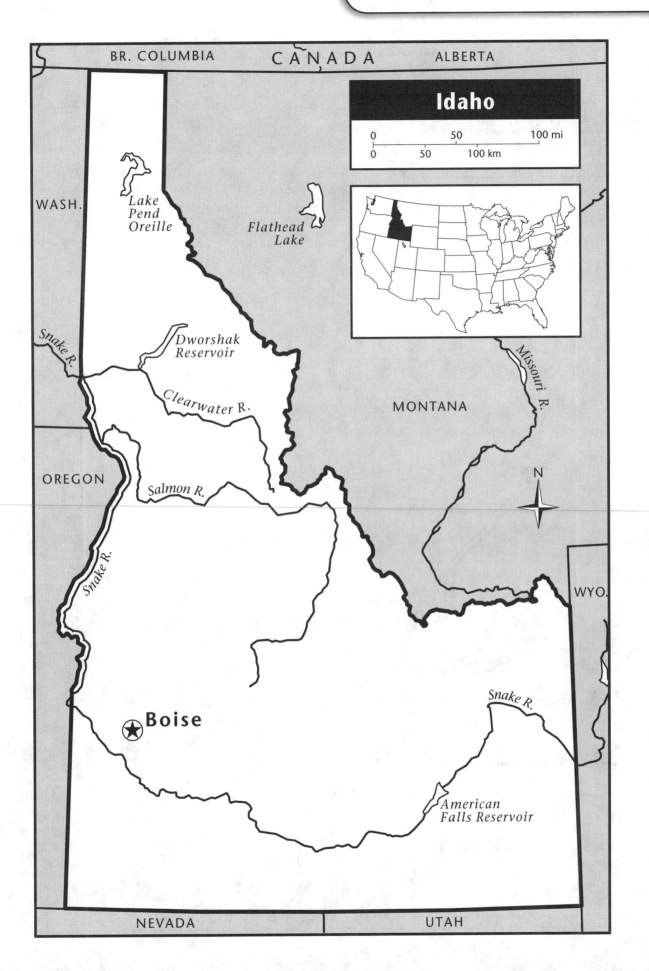

BR. COLUMBIA · CANADA · ALBERTA

Idaho

0   50   100 mi
0   50   100 km

WASH.

Lake Pend Oreille

Flathead Lake

Snake R.

Dworshak Reservoir

Clearwater R.

MONTANA

Missouri R.

OREGON

Salmon R.

N

Snake R.

WYO.

★ **Boise**

Snake R.

American Falls Reservoir

NEVADA   UTAH

25

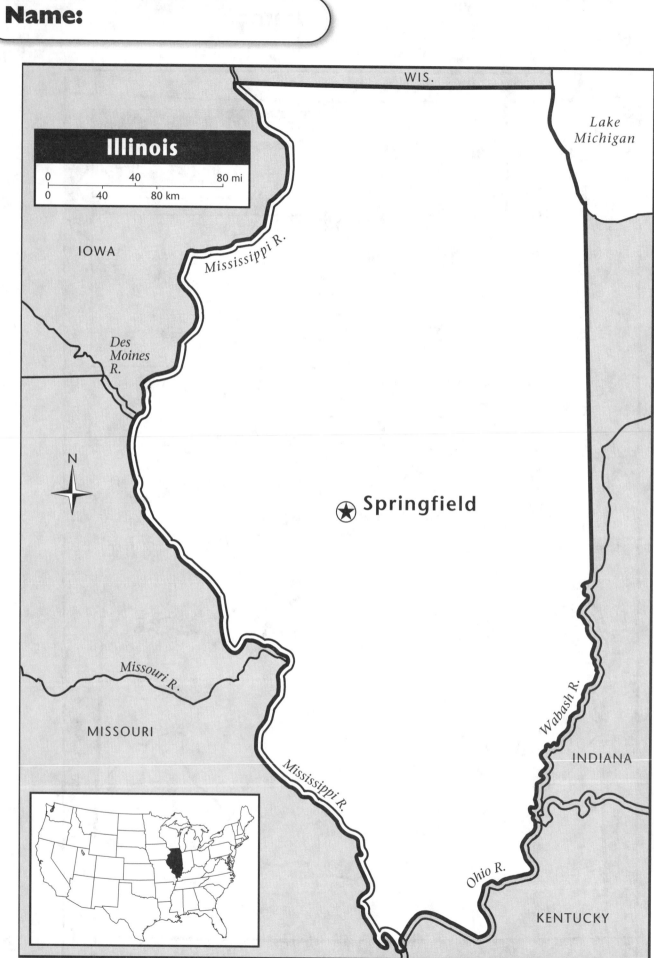

Illinois

0   40   80 mi
0   40   80 km

WIS.

Lake Michigan

IOWA

Mississippi R.

Des Moines R.

N

Springfield

Missouri R.

MISSOURI

Mississippi R.

Wabash R.

INDIANA

Ohio R.

KENTUCKY

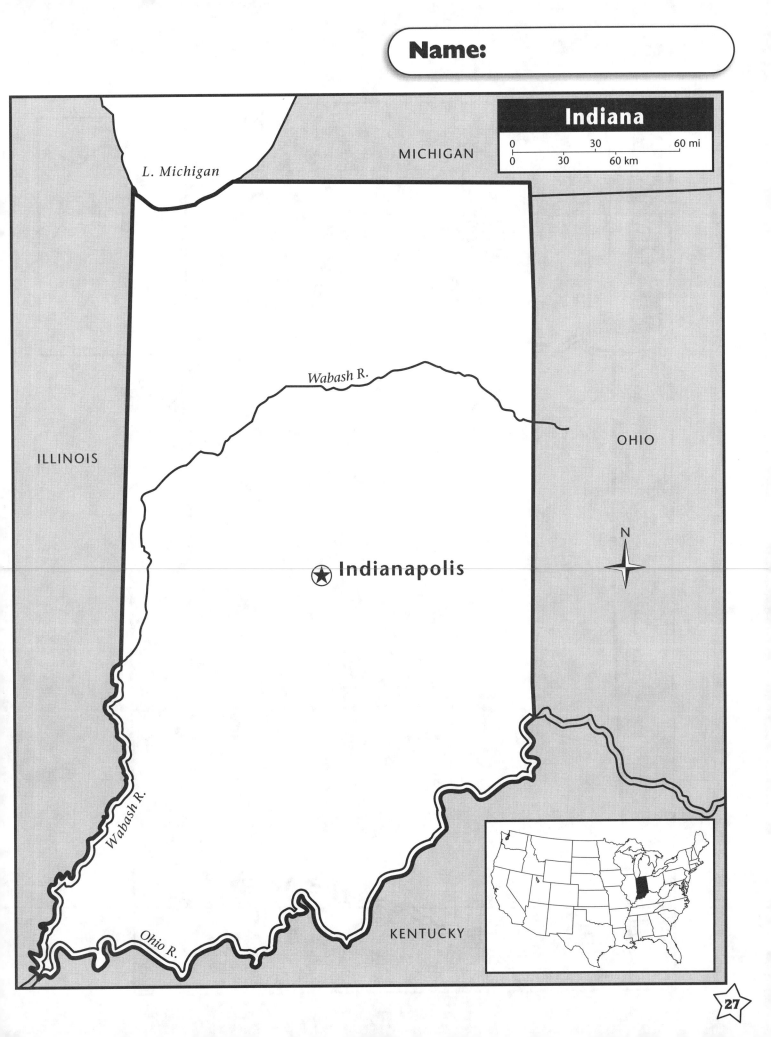

Indiana

0	30	60 mi
0	30	60 km

MICHIGAN

L. Michigan

Wabash R.

ILLINOIS

OHIO

N

⭐ **Indianapolis**

Wabash R.

Ohio R.

KENTUCKY

27

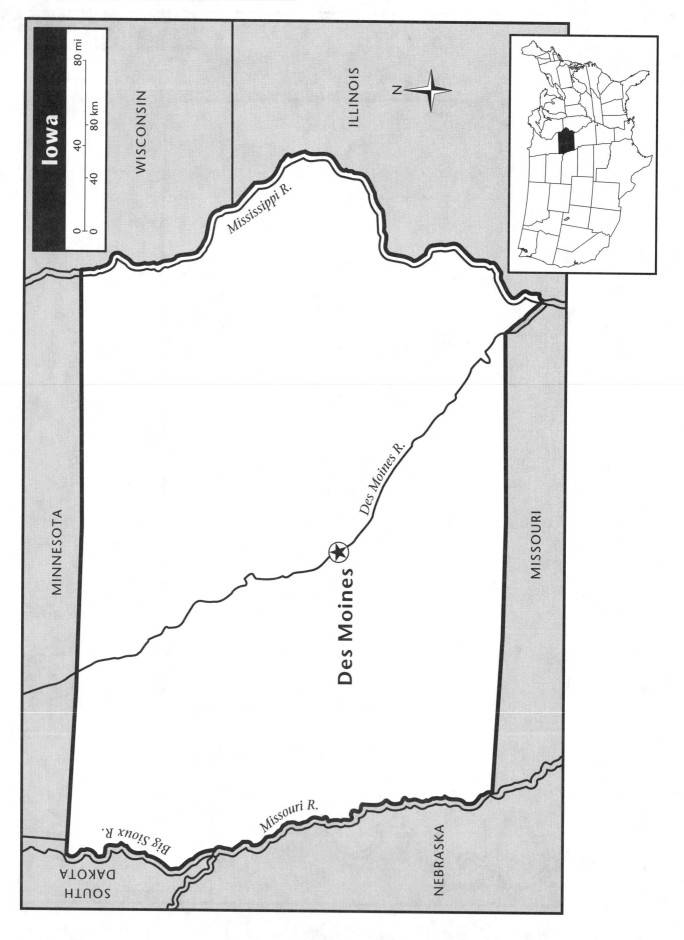

Iowa

80 mi

80 km
40   40

40   40
0   0

WISCONSIN

ILLINOIS

N

Mississippi R.

MINNESOTA

Des Moines R.

⊛ **Des Moines**

MISSOURI

Missouri R.

Big Sioux R.

SOUTH DAKOTA

NEBRASKA

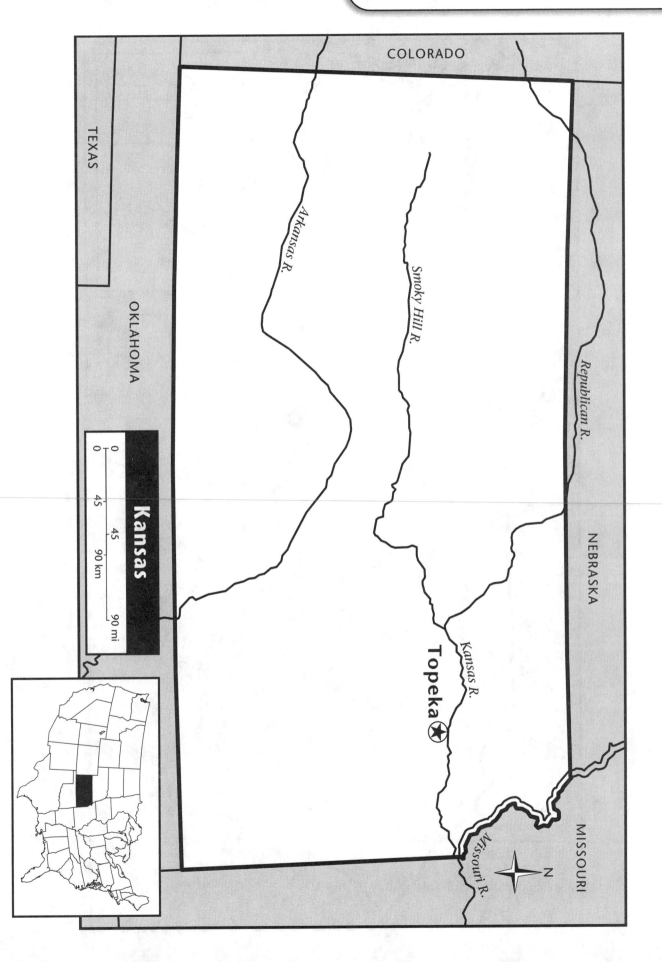

COLORADO

TEXAS

OKLAHOMA

Arkansas R.

Smoky Hill R.

Republican R.

NEBRASKA

Kansas

0
0
45
45
90 km
90 mi

Topeka ★

Kansas R.

Missouri R.

MISSOURI

N

29

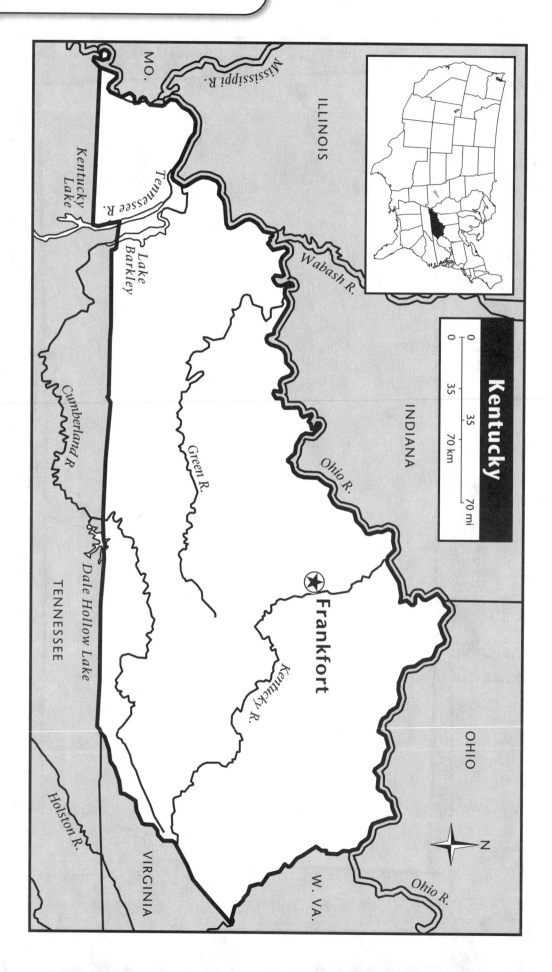

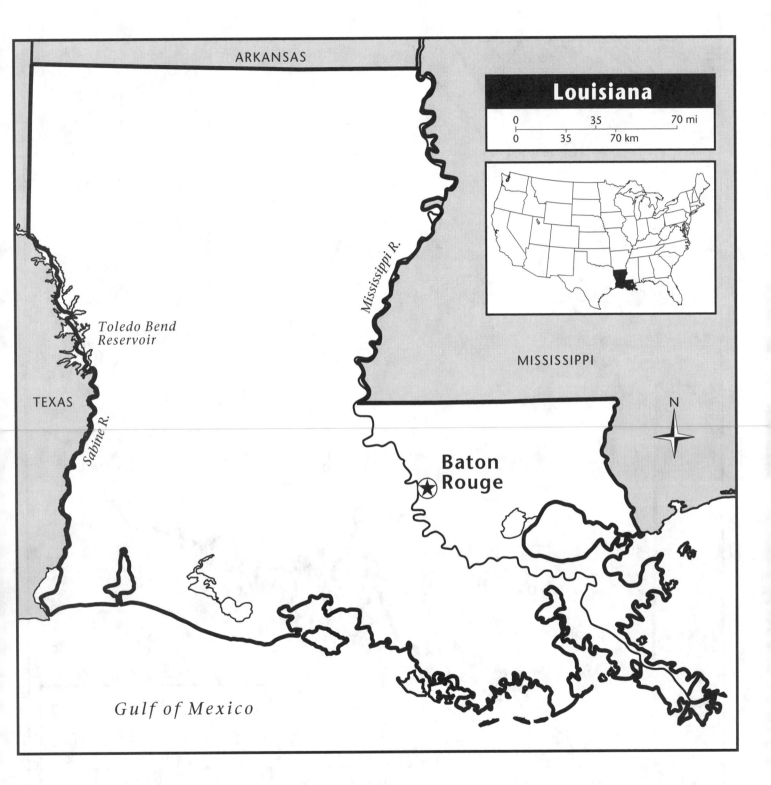

ARKANSAS

Louisiana

| 0 | | 35 | | 70 mi |
| 0 | 35 | | 70 km | |

Toledo Bend
Reservoir

TEXAS

Sabine R.

Mississippi R.

MISSISSIPPI

N

Baton
Rouge

Gulf of Mexico

31

Maine

0   30   60 mi
0   30   60 km

St. Lawrence R.

CANADA

QUEBEC

Penobscot R.

NEW
BRUNSWICK

Saint John R.

Grand
Lake

Augusta ⭐

N

N.H.

ATLANTIC
OCEAN

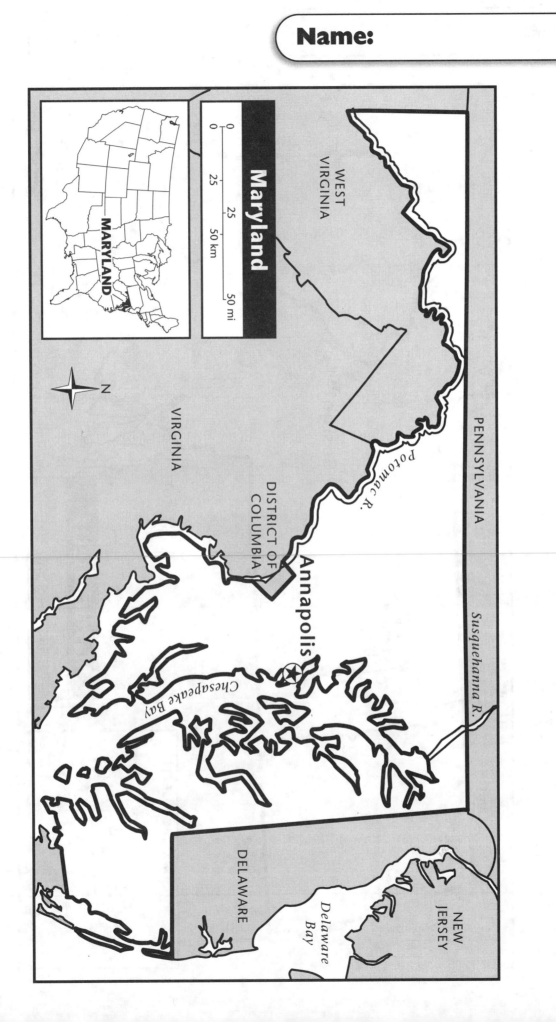

Maryland

WEST VIRGINIA

VIRGINIA

PENNSYLVANIA

Potomac R.

Susquehanna R.

DISTRICT OF COLUMBIA

Annapolis

Chesapeake Bay

DELAWARE

Delaware Bay

NEW JERSEY

MARYLAND

N

0 25 50 km
0 25 50 mi

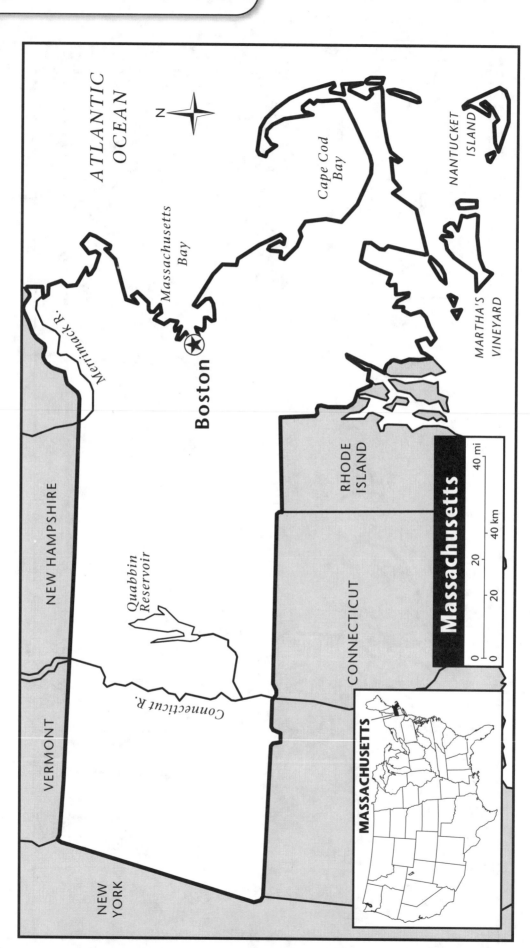

ATLANTIC OCEAN

N

Cape Cod Bay

NANTUCKET ISLAND

Massachusetts Bay

MARTHA'S VINEYARD

Merrimack R.

Boston

NEW HAMPSHIRE

Quabbin Reservoir

RHODE ISLAND

Connecticut R.

CONNECTICUT

VERMONT

Massachusetts

0   20   40 km
0   20   40 mi

NEW YORK

MASSACHUSETTS

KEWEENAW
PENINSULA

Lake Superior

C A N A D A

ONTARIO

Menominee R.

Wisconsin R.

Green Bay

WISCONSIN

*Lake
Huron*

*L.
Winnebago*

*Lake
Michigan*

Saginaw Bay

Muskegon R.

Michigan

0		50		100 mi
0	50		100 km	

Grand R.

⊛ **Lansing**

INDIANA

OHIO

*Lake
Erie*

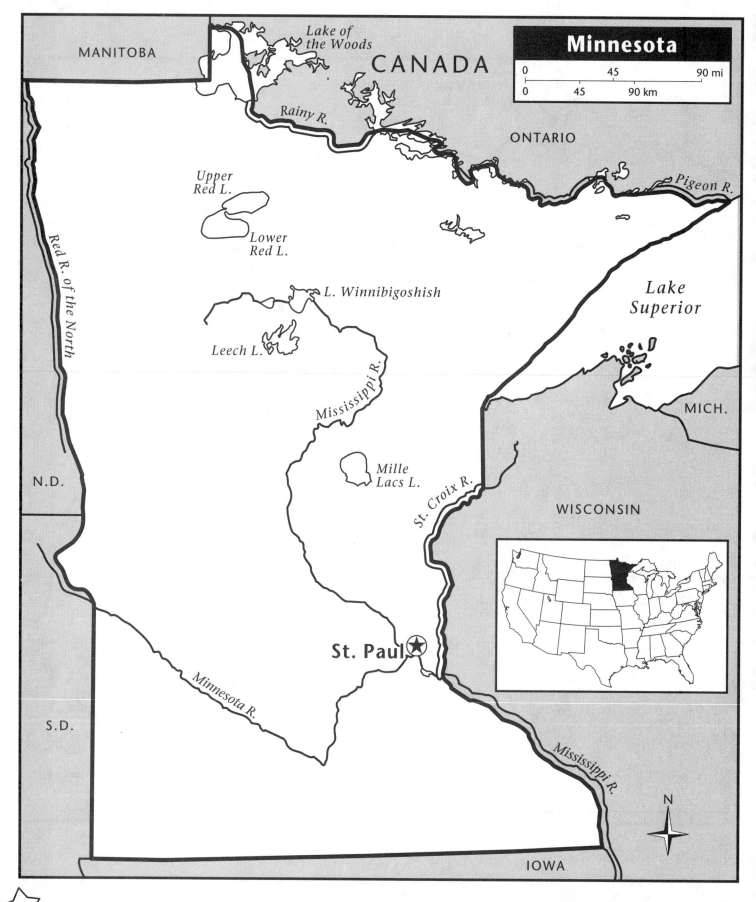

MANITOBA

CANADA

Lake of the Woods

Rainy R.

ONTARIO

Minnesota

0   45   90 mi

0   45   90 km

Pigeon R.

Upper Red L.

Lower Red L.

Red R. of the North

L. Winnibigoshish

Lake Superior

Leech L.

MICH.

Mississippi R.

N.D.

Mille Lacs L.

St. Croix R.

WISCONSIN

St. Paul ★

Minnesota R.

S.D.

Mississippi R.

N

IOWA

Mississippi

| 0 | 35 | 70 mi |
| 0 | 35 | 70 km |

TENNESSEE

ARKANSAS

N

Pearl R.

ALA.

⭐ Jackson

LOUISIANA

Mississippi R.

Gulf
of
Mexico

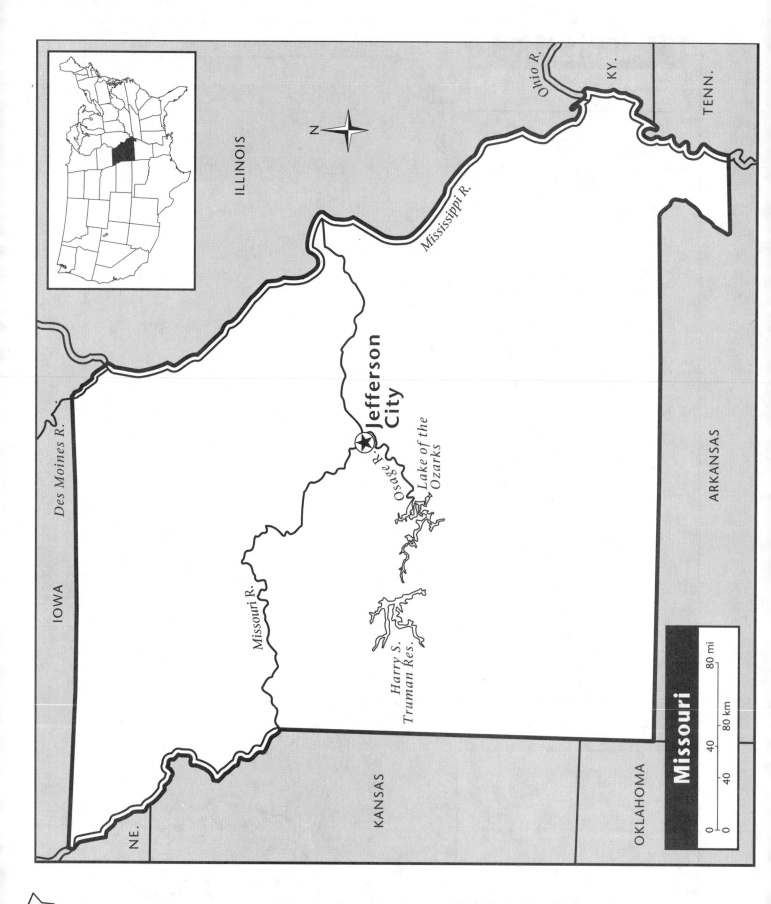

ILLINOIS

N

Ohio R.

KY.

TENN.

Mississippi R.

Jefferson City

Des Moines R.

Osage R.

Lake of the Ozarks

ARKANSAS

IOWA

Missouri R.

Harry S. Truman Res.

KANSAS

OKLAHOMA

N.E.

Missouri

80 mi

80 km

40

40

0

0

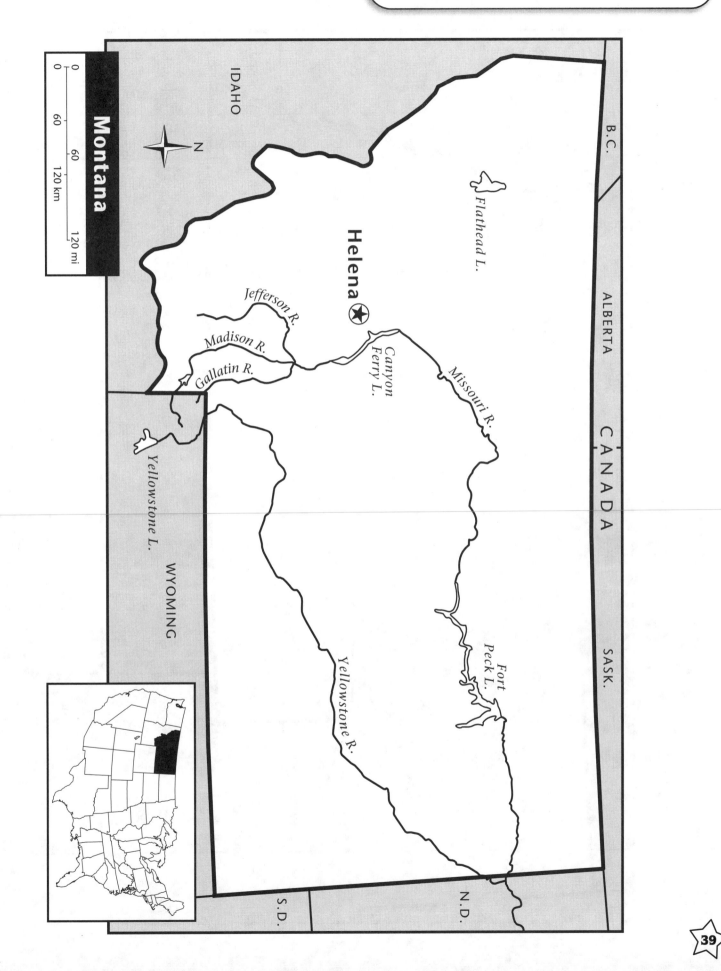

Montana

IDAHO

B.C.

ALBERTA

CANADA

SASK.

N.D.

S.D.

WYOMING

Flathead L.

Helena

Jefferson R.

Madison R.

Gallatin R.

Yellowstone L.

Canyon Ferry L.

Missouri R.

Fort Peck L.

Yellowstone R.

N

0 60 120 km
0 60 120 mi

39

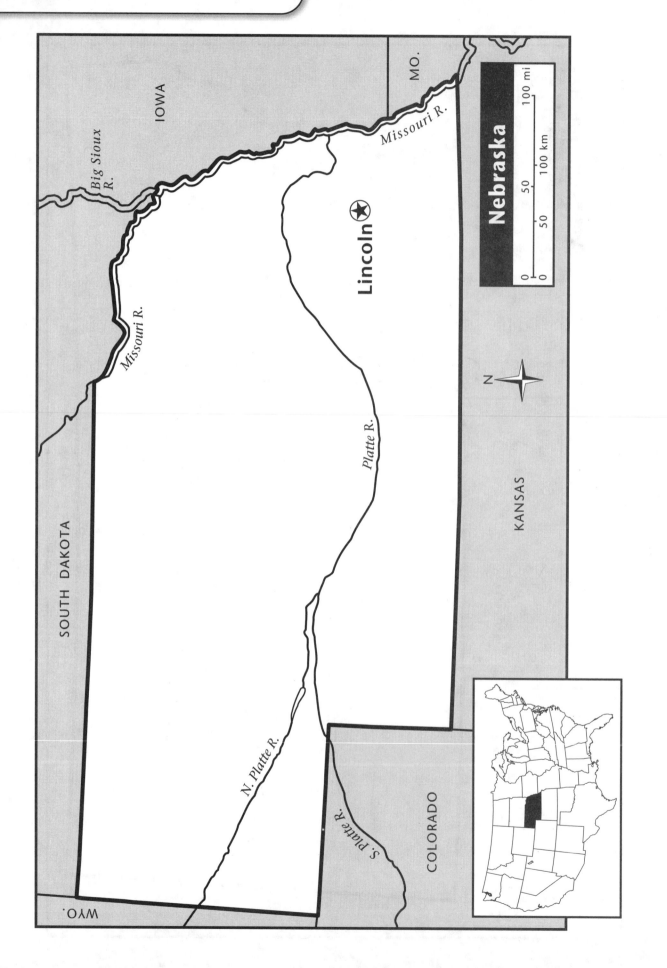

Nebraska

100 mi
50
0

100 km
50
0

N

MO.

Missouri R.

IOWA

Big Sioux R.

Lincoln ⭐

Missouri R.

SOUTH DAKOTA

Platte R.

KANSAS

N. Platte R.

S. Platte R.

COLORADO

WYO.

40

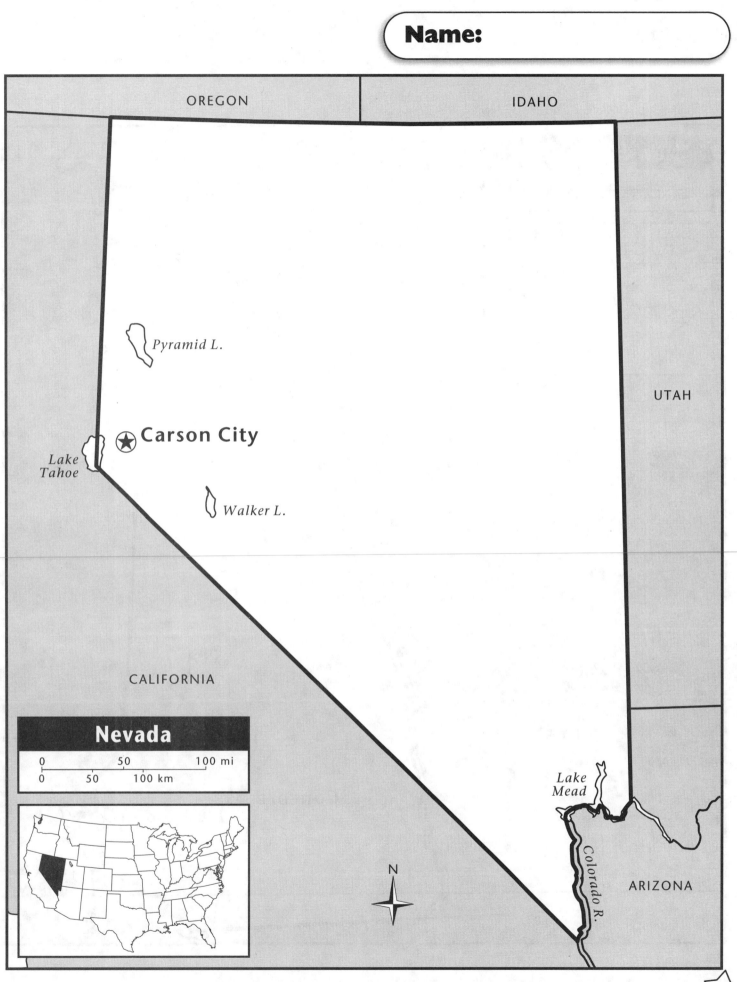

OREGON

IDAHO

UTAH

Pyramid L.

⭐ **Carson City**

*Lake
Tahoe*

Walker L.

CALIFORNIA

Nevada

0		50		100 mi
0	50		100 km	

*Lake
Mead*

N

ARIZONA

Colorado R.

41

New Hampshire

0   20   40 mi
0   20   40 km

NEW HAMPSHIRE

CANADA

QUEBEC

Lac Memphrémagog

Umbagog Lake

NEW YORK

Lake Champlain

MAINE

VERMONT

Connecticut R.

Lake George

Lake Winnipesaukee

Concord ★

N

Great Bay

Merrimac R.

ATLANTIC OCEAN

MASS.

Name:

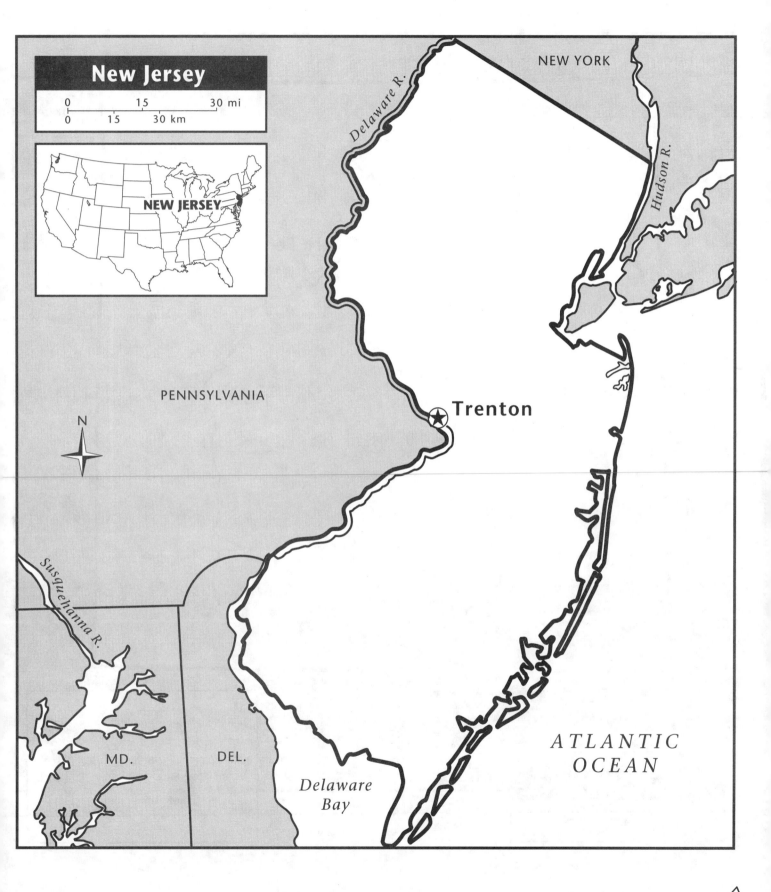

New Jersey

0   15   30 mi
0   15   30 km

NEW JERSEY

NEW YORK

Delaware R.

Hudson R.

PENNSYLVANIA

N

★ Trenton

Susquehanna R.

MD.

DEL.

Delaware
Bay

ATLANTIC
OCEAN

43

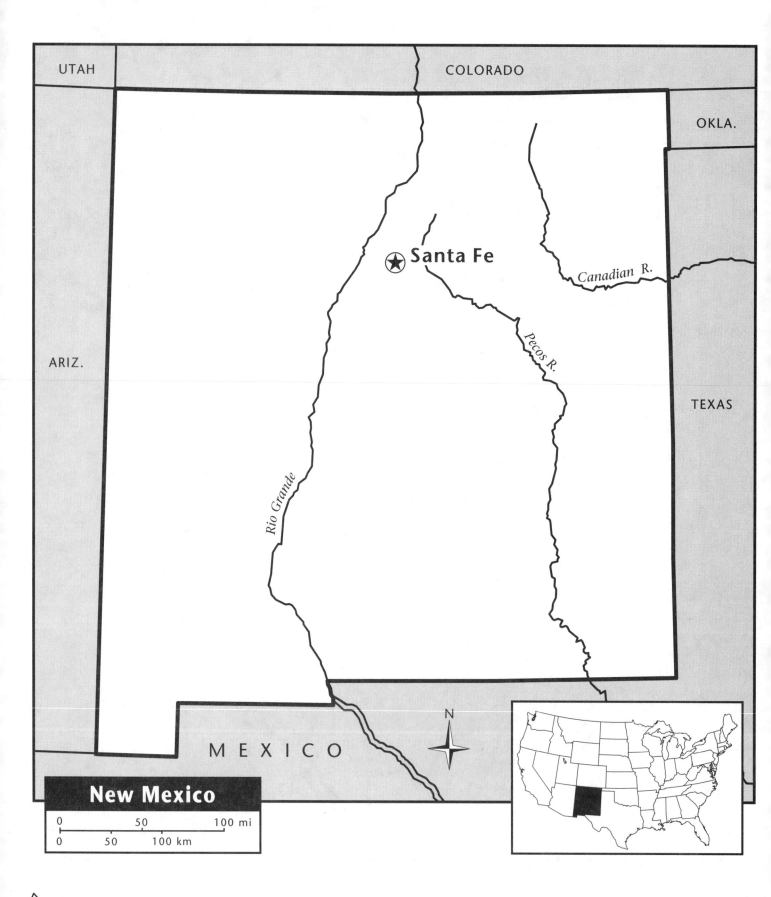

UTAH

COLORADO

OKLA.

ARIZ.

★ **Santa Fe**

Canadian R.

Pecos R.

TEXAS

Rio Grande

M E X I C O

N

New Mexico

0		50		100 mi

0	50	100 km

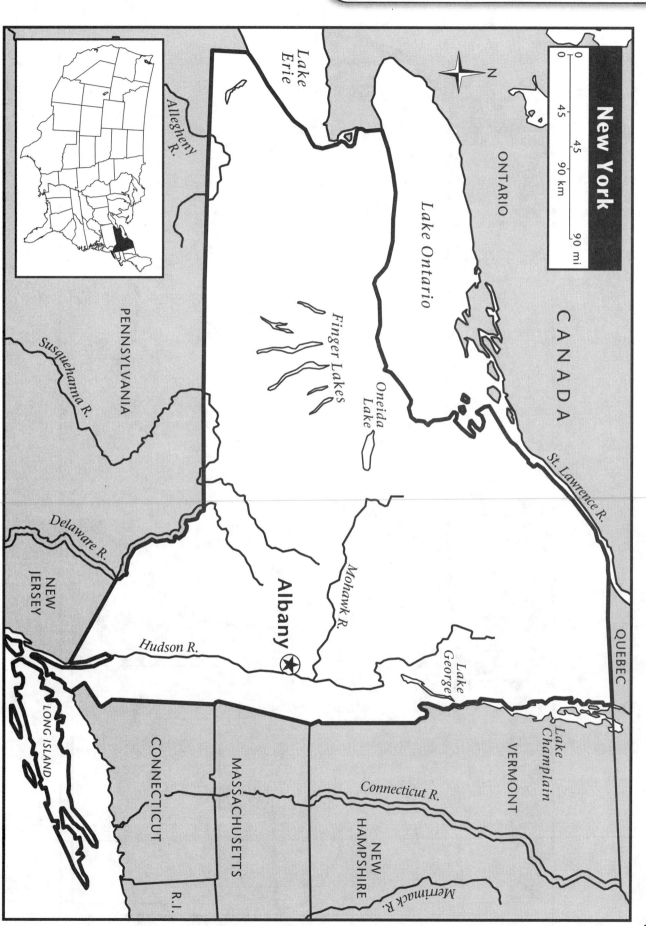

New York

Lake Erie

Allegheny R.

ONTARIO

N

New York

0   45   90 km
0   45   90 mi

CANADA

Lake Ontario

PENNSYLVANIA

Susquehanna R.

Finger Lakes

Oneida Lake

St. Lawrence R.

Delaware R.

NEW JERSEY

Albany

Mohawk R.

QUEBEC

Hudson R.

Lake George

Lake Champlain

VERMONT

LONG ISLAND

CONNECTICUT

MASSACHUSETTS

Connecticut R.

NEW HAMPSHIRE

Merrimack R.

R.I.

45

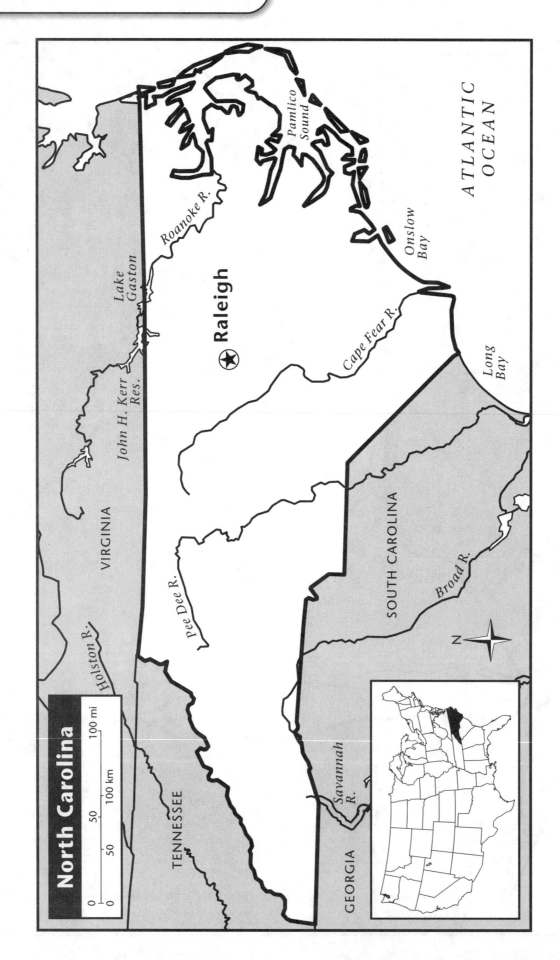

North Carolina

Scale: 0 50 100 mi / 0 50 100 km

ATLANTIC OCEAN

Pamlico Sound

Onslow Bay

Long Bay

Roanoke R.

Lake Gaston

★ Raleigh

Cape Fear R.

John H. Kerr Res.

VIRGINIA

SOUTH CAROLINA

Broad R.

Pee Dee R.

Holston R.

TENNESSEE

Savannah R.

GEORGIA

N

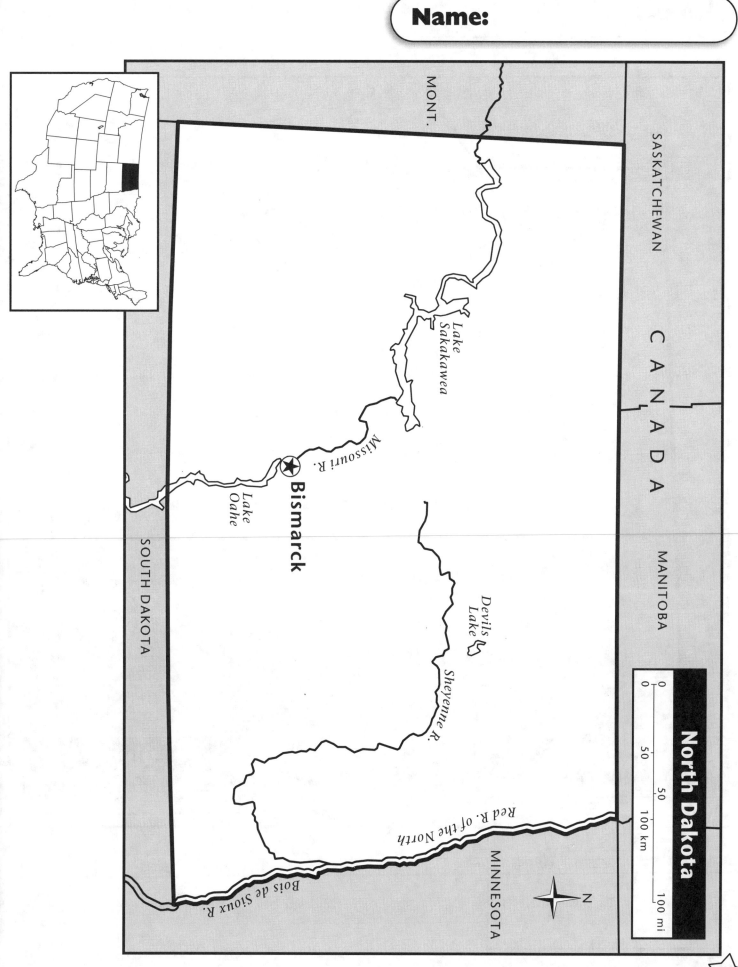

North Dakota

MONT.

SASKATCHEWAN

C A N A D A

MANITOBA

Lake
Sakakawea

Missouri R.

Bismarck

Lake
Oahe

SOUTH DAKOTA

Devils
Lake

Sheyenne R.

Red R. of the North

Bois de Sioux R.

MINNESOTA

N

0   50   100 km
0   50   100 mi

Name:

CANADA

MICHIGAN

PA.

Sandusky R.

IND.

⭐ **Columbus**

Ohio R.

WEST VIRGINIA

N

Ohio R.

KENTUCKY

Ohio

| 0 | 30 | 60 mi |
| 0 | 30 | 60 km |

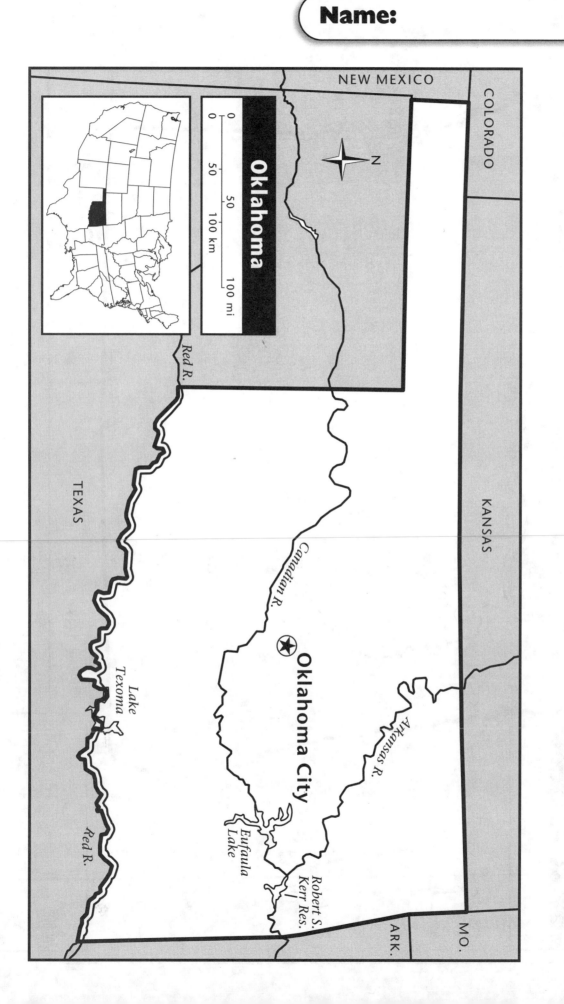

Oklahoma

NEW MEXICO

COLORADO

KANSAS

TEXAS

Red R.

Canadian R.

Oklahoma City

Lake Texoma

Eufaula Lake

Arkansas R.

Robert S. Kerr Res.

Red R.

ARK.

MO.

0
0
50
50
100 km
100 mi

49

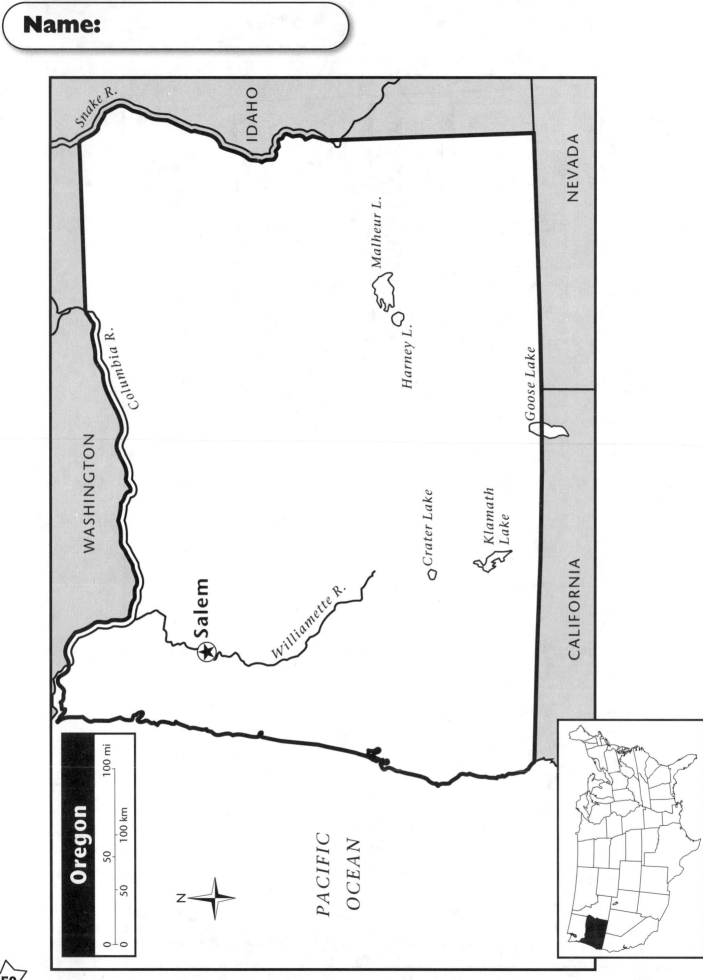

Oregon

100 mi
100 km
50
50
50
0
0

N

PACIFIC OCEAN

Snake R.

IDAHO

NEVADA

Malheur L.

Harney L.

Goose Lake

Columbia R.

WASHINGTON

Crater Lake

Klamath Lake

CALIFORNIA

Salem

Williamette R.

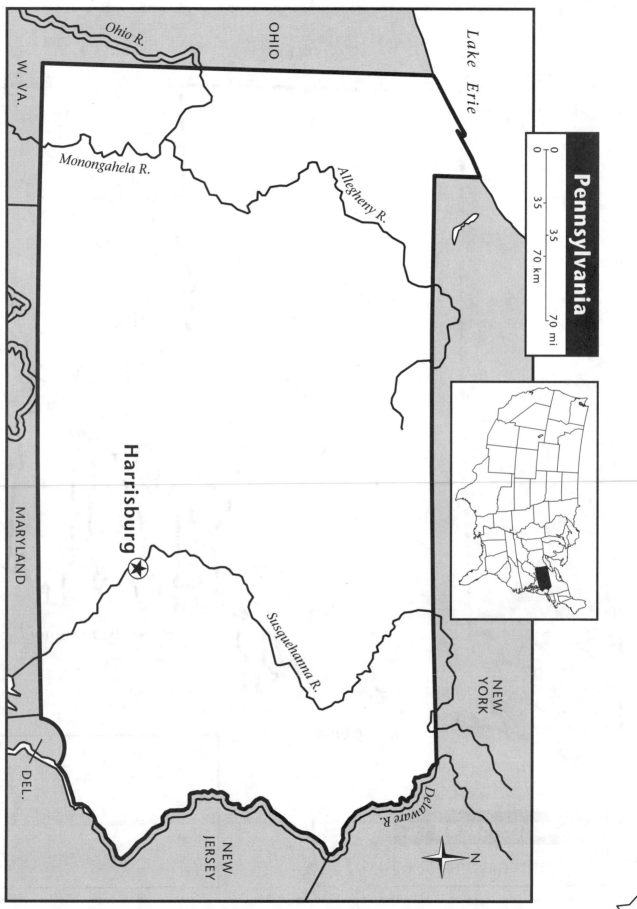

Pennsylvania

0 35 70 km
0 35 70 mi

Ohio R.

OHIO

Lake Erie

W. VA.

Monongahela R.

Allegheny R.

MARYLAND

Harrisburg

Susquehanna R.

DEL.

NEW JERSEY

NEW YORK

Delaware R.

N

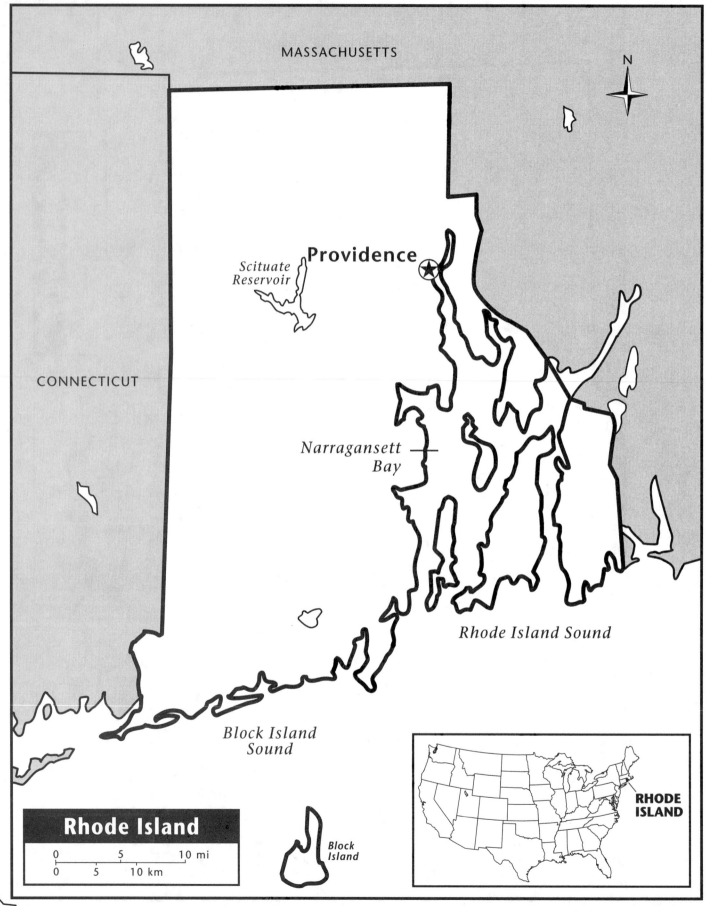

MASSACHUSETTS

N

CONNECTICUT

Scituate Reservoir

Providence

Narragansett Bay

Rhode Island Sound

Block Island Sound

Rhode Island

| 0 | | 5 | | 10 mi |
| 0 | 5 | | 10 km | |

Block Island

RHODE ISLAND

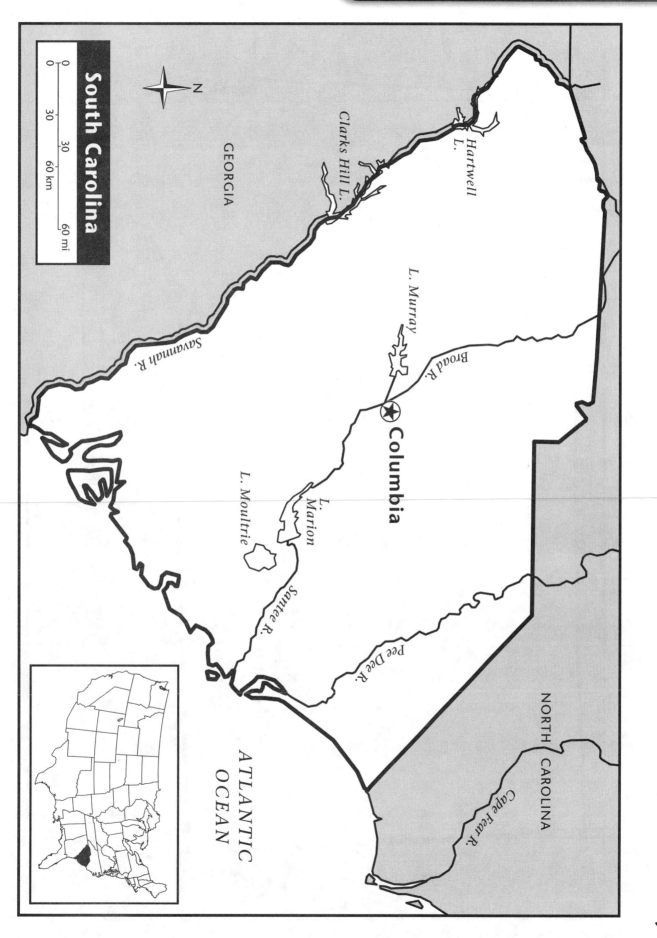

South Carolina

0
0
30
30
60 km
60 mi

N

GEORGIA

Clarks Hill L.

Hartwell L.

L. Murray

Broad R.

Columbia

Savannah R.

L. Moultrie

L. Marion

Santee R.

Pee Dee R.

ATLANTIC OCEAN

NORTH CAROLINA

Cape Fear R.

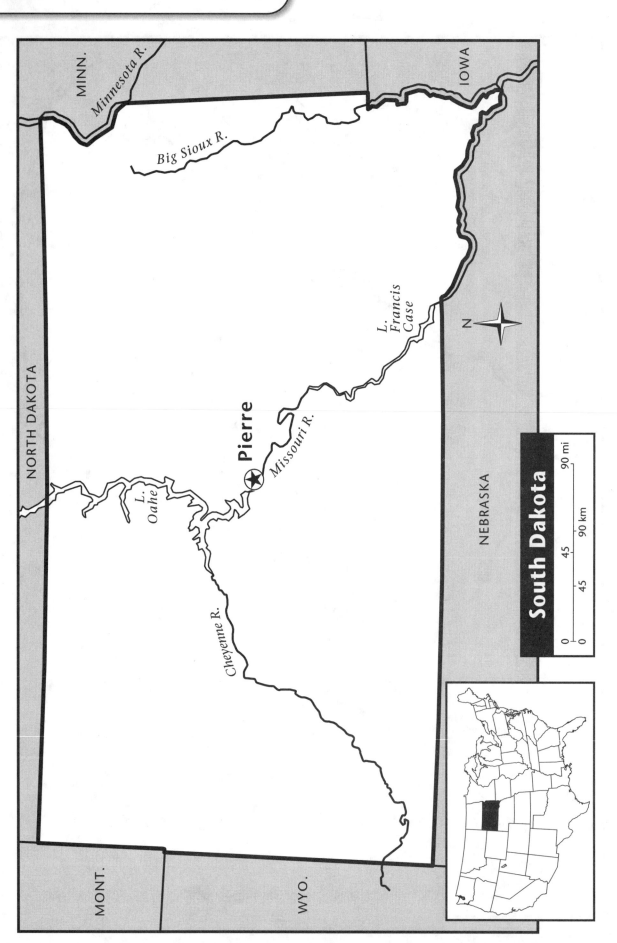

MINN.

Minnesota R.

IOWA

Big Sioux R.

NORTH DAKOTA

L. Francis Case

N

Pierre

Missouri R.

L. Oahe

NEBRASKA

South Dakota

0   45   90 mi

0   45   90 km

Cheyenne R.

MONT.

WYO.

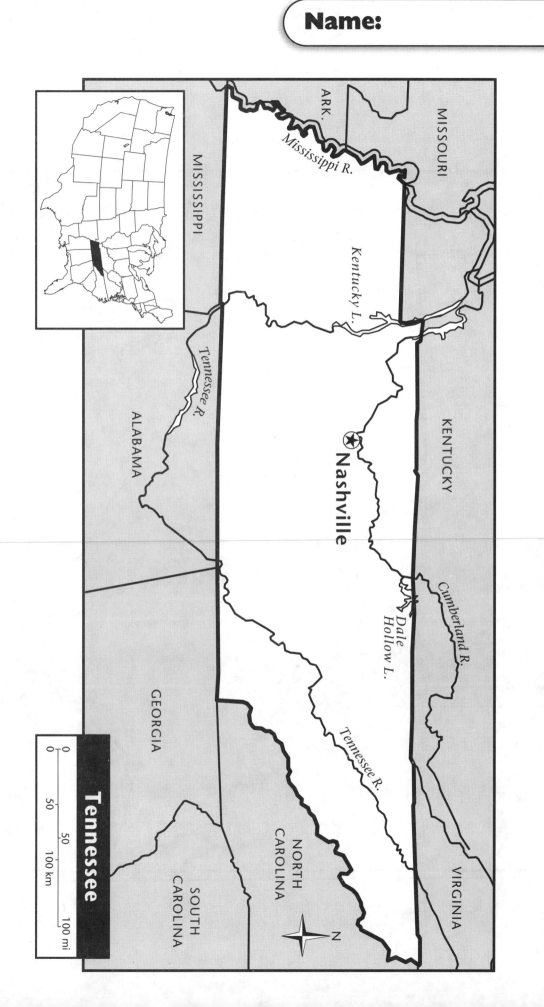

Tennessee

MISSISSIPPI

ARK.

MISSOURI

Mississippi R.

Kentucky L.

KENTUCKY

Tennessee R.

ALABAMA

Nashville

Dale Hollow L.

Cumberland R.

Tennessee R.

GEORGIA

NORTH CAROLINA

SOUTH CAROLINA

VIRGINIA

N

0 50 100 km
0 50 100 mi

55

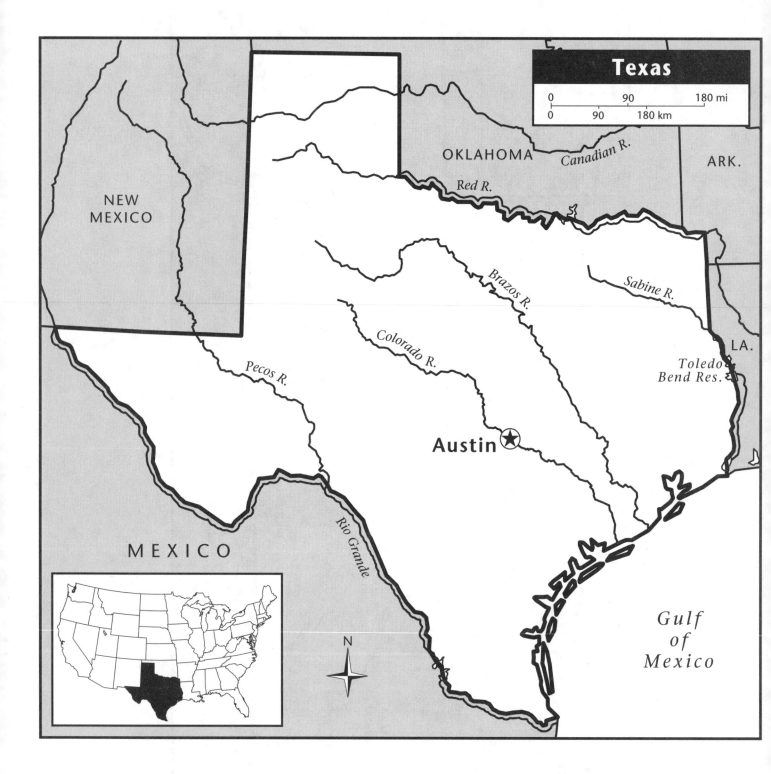

Texas

| 0 | 90 | 180 mi |
| 0 | 90 | 180 km |

NEW MEXICO

OKLAHOMA

Canadian R.

ARK.

Red R.

Brazos R.

Sabine R.

Colorado R.

LA.

Pecos R.

Toledo Bend Res.

Austin ★

MEXICO

Rio Grande

N

Gulf
of
Mexico

Utah

Great Salt Lake

★ **Salt Lake City**

Utah Lake

IDAHO

WYOMING

Flaming Gorge Res.

Green R.

Colorado R.

L. Powell

NEVADA

COLORADO

ARIZONA

N.M.

N

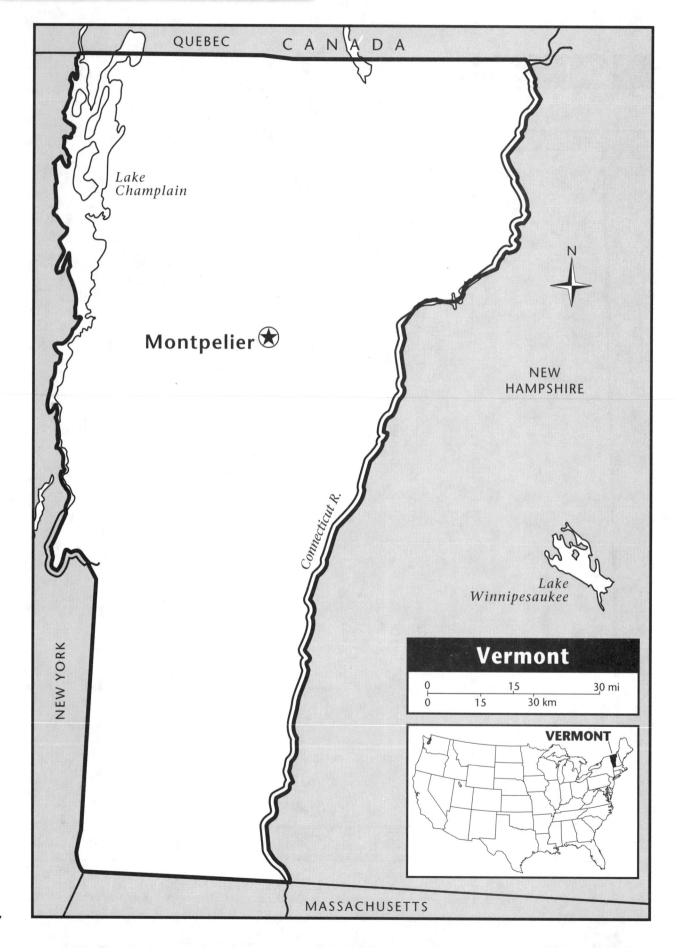

QUEBEC CANADA

Lake Champlain

Montpelier ★

Connecticut R.

N

NEW HAMPSHIRE

Lake Winnipesaukee

NEW YORK

Vermont

0	15	30 mi
0	15	30 km

VERMONT

MASSACHUSETTS

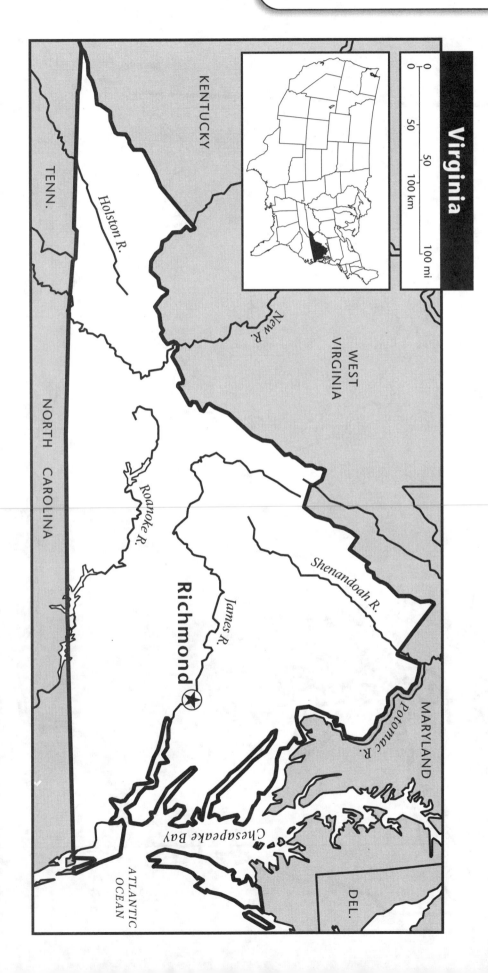

Virginia

KENTUCKY

TENN.

Holston R.

NORTH CAROLINA

Roanoke R.

Richmond ✪

James R.

New R.

WEST VIRGINIA

Shenandoah R.

Potomac R.

MARYLAND

Chesapeake Bay

ATLANTIC OCEAN

DEL.

0   50   100 km
0   50   100 mi

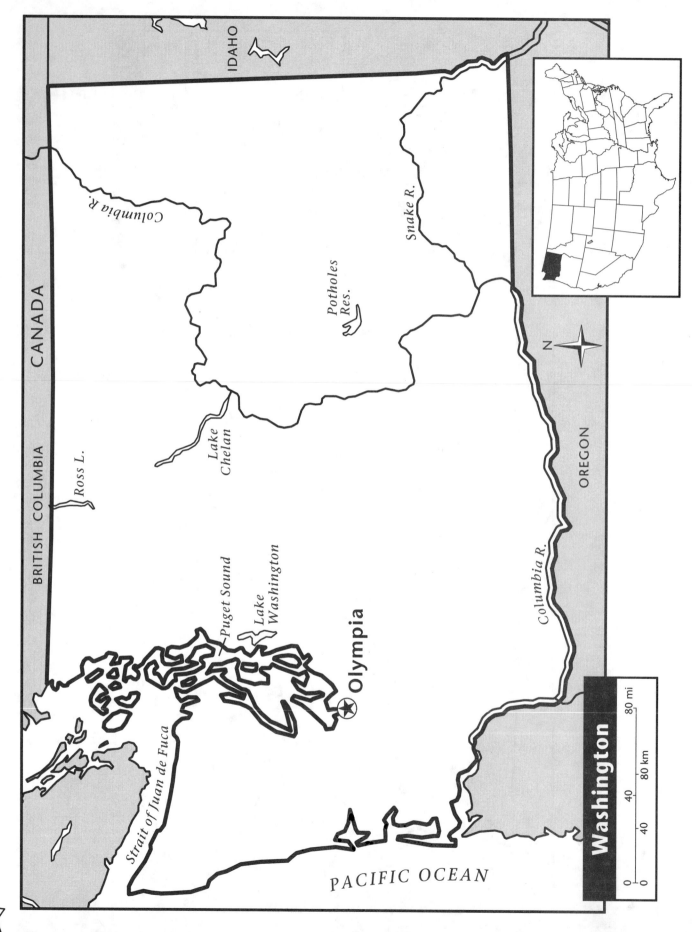

IDAHO

CANADA

BRITISH COLUMBIA

Columbia R.

Ross L.

Snake R.

Potholes Res.

Lake Chelan

N

OREGON

Puget Sound

Lake Washington

Olympia

Columbia R.

Strait of Juan de Fuca

PACIFIC OCEAN

Washington

80 mi

40   80 km

40

0   0

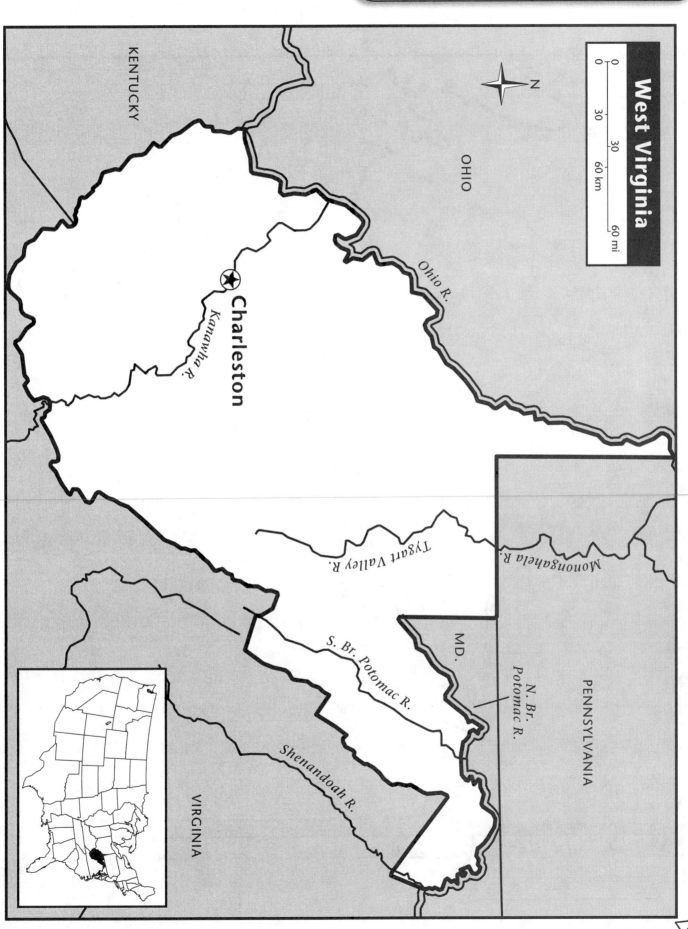

West Virginia

0 30 60 km
0 30 60 mi

N

KENTUCKY

OHIO

Ohio R.

Charleston

Kanawha R.

Tygart Valley R.

Monongahela R.

S. Br. Potomac R.

MD.

N. Br. Potomac R.

PENNSYLVANIA

Shenandoah R.

VIRGINIA

61

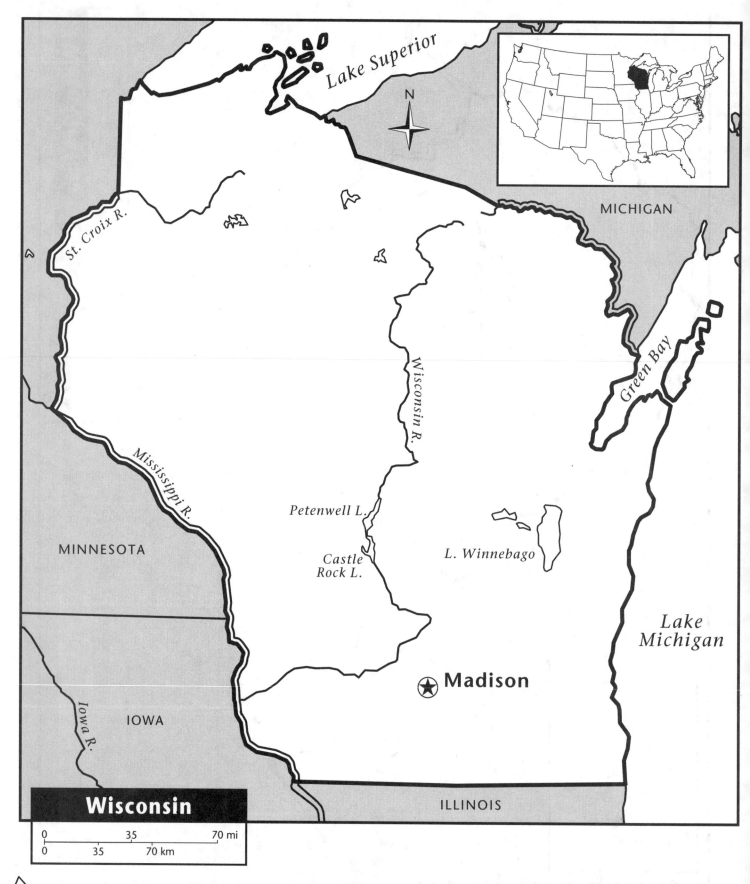

MICHIGAN

Lake Superior

N

St. Croix R.

MINNESOTA

Mississippi R.

Wisconsin R.

Green Bay

Petenwell L.

Castle
Rock L.

L. Winnebago

IOWA

Iowa R.

Lake
Michigan

⭐ **Madison**

Wisconsin

ILLINOIS

| 0 | 35 | 70 mi |
| 0 | 35 | 70 km |

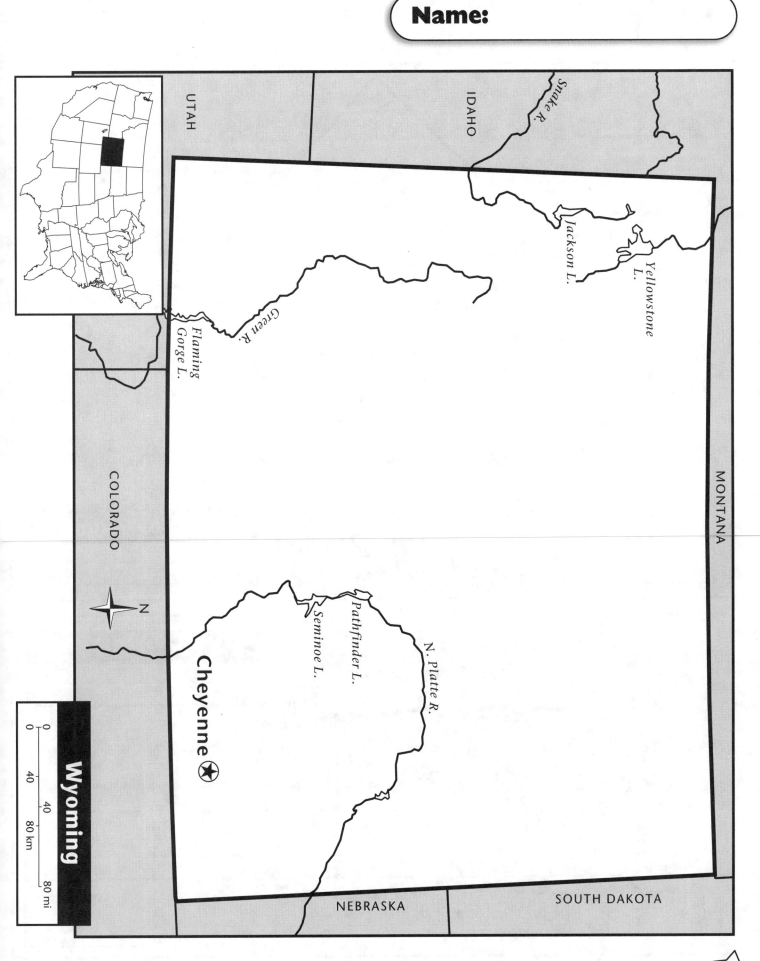

UTAH

IDAHO

Snake R.

Jackson L.

Yellowstone L.

Green R.

Flaming Gorge L.

MONTANA

COLORADO

N

Cheyenne ⊛

Seminoe L.

Pathfinder L.

N. Platte R.

Wyoming

0
0
40
40
40
40
80 km
80 mi

NEBRASKA

SOUTH DAKOTA

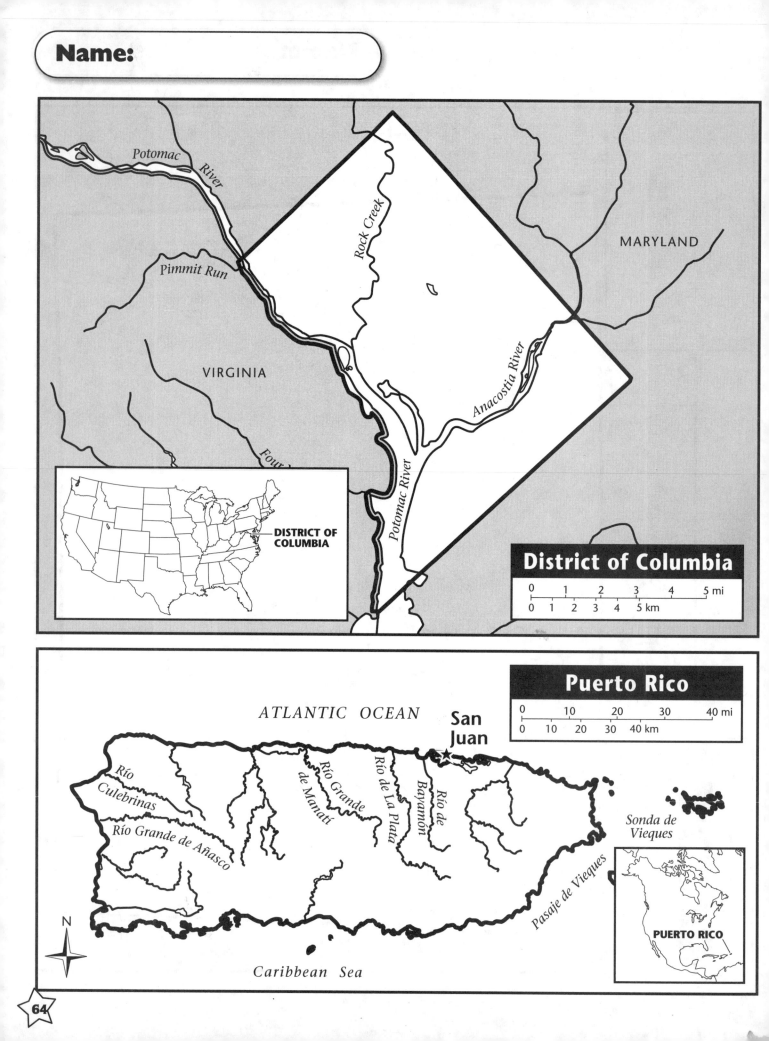

Potomac River

Rock Creek

MARYLAND

Pimmit Run

Anacostia River

VIRGINIA

Potomac River

Four

DISTRICT OF
COLUMBIA

District of Columbia

| 0 | 1 | 2 | 3 | 4 | 5 mi |
| 0 | 1 | 2 | 3 | 4 | 5 km |

Puerto Rico

| 0 | 10 | 20 | 30 | 40 mi |
| 0 | 10 | 20 | 30 | 40 km |

ATLANTIC OCEAN

San Juan

Río Culebrinas

Río de Manatí

Río Grande

Río de La Plata

Río de Bayamón

Sonda de Vieques

Río Grande de Añasco

Pasaje de Vieques

PUERTO RICO

N

Caribbean Sea